6 ⁰⁰

50 hikes

IN MOUNT RAINIER
NATIONAL PARK

Text: Ira Spring and Harvey Manning
Photos: Bob and Ira Spring
Maps: Marge Mueller

THE MOUNTAINEERS · SEATTLE
with The Mount Rainier Natural History Association

Second edition

The Mountaineers: Organized 1906 "...to explore, study, preserve and enjoy the natural beauty of the Northwest."

Published by The Mountaineers, 715 Pike Street
Seattle, Washington 98101

Published simultaneously in Canada by
Douglas & McIntyre Ltd., 1615 Venables Street
Vancouver, British Columbia V5L 2H1

Manufactured in the United States of America
First edition, June 1969
Second edition, June 1978; second printing, October 1980;
third printing, March 1982

Library of Congress Catalog Card No. 78-84752
ISBN 0-916890-19-8

Cover photo: Mount Rainier from Dege Peak, Hike 24
Title photo: Mount Rainier reflected in alpine tarn at Moraine Park, Hike 18

Avalanche lilies on Mazama Ridge

FOREWORD

One of the best ways to savor Mount Rainier is from the trails. You can see the mountain from many different angles and discover its moods and disguises. The peak is like an old-fashioned kaleidoscope. It looks like a different mountain from one side to another. The more you see of it, the more its variety will impress you. You will soon know why native Americans held the peak in such awe and why Northwest citizens all claim it as their own.

We hope you will take some hikes and discover some personal places. For those of you who don't have the time to hike the entire 300 miles of trail in the Park, **50 Hikes in Mount Rainier** will give you a chance to decide which hikes are best for you. There are many new views of the mountain awaiting you around the next bend in the trail, as well as new flowerfields, waterfalls, glaciers, deep forests, and perhaps an elusive mountain goat. Take the trail of your choice and discover your own Mount Rainier. Good hiking!

May 1978
William J. Briggle, Superintendent
Mount Rainier National Park

5

INTRODUCTION

The National Park Act of 1916 declares that the purpose of Mount Rainier National Park is "to conserve the scenery and the natural and historic objects and the wildlife . . . " Each visitor must therefore enjoy the Park "in such manner and by such means as will leave it unimpaired for the enjoyment of future generations." A good motto for Park users is: "Take only a picture. Leave only a footprint."

The first National Parks were set aside in an era when frontier country was being recklessly exploited by "today" men equally unaware of yesterday and tomorrow. Even then, however, when empty lands seemed inexhaustible, some Americans recognized that certain climaxes of the scenery were too precious to be left open to wanton desecration; thus it was, in 1899, that Mount Rainier National Park was established.

Now, as in the beginning of the concept, a National Park is the highest protection Americans give their land, the purest expression of a nature-sensitive ethic. Ultimately, the "ecological conscience" must be extended to all remaining wildlands in this nation and every other—and indeed to the entire rural and suburban and urban world. In the National Parks a citizenry still retaining many habits of the frontier can learn the sort of behavior required on a planet that has more people and a more violent technology each passing year.

More Information

All trails in this book are administered by the National Park Service. For further information write:

Mt. Rainier National Park
Ashford, Washington 98304

Or call:

(206) 569-2211

Trails

On the whole, Mount Rainier National Park has the best-built and best-maintained trails of any area in Washington, offering many miles of wide, smooth paths. Conditions are especially good in forests; in alpine meadows, where the short season makes maintenance difficult, the tread is sometimes sketchy.

As soon as the snow melts, trail crews cut away fallen trees and repair winter damage. River crossings are the worst problem. The glacial streams flood and change course and wash out bridges with exasperating frequency. Much of the flooding occurs in June, and it may be mid-July before all the bridges are replaced. If planning a hike before that date, be sure to find out at a Park entrance or ranger station whether the necessary bridges are in place.

The Mount Rainier contour maps in both the 15-minute and 7½-minute series, as well as in the Green Trails version (available for purchase at map stores and the Park's visitor centers) should be carried and consulted by any party taking a long trip. An accurate lithographed pictorial map of the Park, painted by Dee Molenaar from 1960 aerial photographs, is also available.

Meters or Feet?

In anticipation of the day when the last diehard hikers, loyalists to the English system, submit to the international conspiracy and accept the metric system, but also to ease the transition period when some Park signs have not yet been converted, measurements in this book are given in both.

Meters or feet, kilometers or miles? Both systems are simple and for trail-measurement purposes neither is better than the other. Americans have gotten along perfectly well for centuries with feet and miles, but then somebody decided it would be fun to make them do it the way the Europeans do. Unless one is an active resister, as many patriots are, it only takes a day or two on the trail to learn the foreign method. Some hikers (those who have spent much time in the Alps and been brainwashed) think it is more fun to hike kilometers than miles because they go whistling by a lot faster. However, gaining 1000 meters of elevation is a lot harder than 1000 feet — more than three times harder, in fact.

Pets

Mount Rainier trails are for people and for the animals who live there. **Pets are not allowed on any trail in the Park.** Wildlife quickly disappears when a dog starts sniffing around—except, maybe, a bear who is angered by the barking and thus becomes a danger to people. The rule against pets covers even the smallest dog or cat, pets on leash, pets carried in arms, and pets walking to one side of the trail and thus technically "not on it." There are no boarding kennels in the Park, so pets should be left at home.

Dogs bother not only wild animals but tame people. Most complaints come from hikers who have been harassed by noisy dogs or have found excrement in their assigned campsites. Rangers are required to give a citation whenever a dog is found in the backcountry.

Horses are allowed on some of the trails in the Park, but their impact on the terrain requires careful management. A party wishing to travel by horse must contact Park headquarters at Ashford to check on the trails that are open to horse use before the trip.

Clothing

Street shoes and city clothing are fine for nature walks and short forest trails, but any long trip—especially at high altitudes—calls for something better. (Hikers arriving at Mount Rainier without proper gear can rent boots and clothing from the guide service at Paradise.)

Sturdy, lug-soled boots are essential for safety and enjoyment on slippery mud and snow, of which Rainier has its share.

Anyone hiking more than an hour from the road must give careful thought to clothing—and the weather. A clear morning is no guarantee it won't be raining by noon, and though being soaked an hour's walk from a dry car is a minor misery in the lowlands, above treeline the experience can be serious.

Mount Rainier makes its own weather, often in a hurry and without warning. Warm sunshine may give way in minutes to a cold, damp fog, and in minutes more to driving rain or snow. A person clothed only for sunshine should turn around and head for home at the first sign of changing weather. Better yet, of course, is to be prepared for the worst by carrying a pack containing a sweater and a hooded windbreaker, raincoat or poncho, and rain pants or chaps.

There is no way to stay dry while hiking in a heavy rain. The maximum hope is to shed some of the water and meanwhile keep warm. Waterproof garments hold the rain out and the perspiration in—the hiker gets wet from the inside. Water-repellent fabric lets the sweat "breathe out"—but after a few hours in a downpour lets the rain leak in. When wearing waterproof or water-repellent garments, it is wise to slow down to avoid overheating.

Some prefer to hike in shorts and T-shirts, getting sopping wet but maintaining warmth by moving at a steady pace; at camp they then put on dry clothing from the pack. If—and only if—one has the dry clothing, this is a good method, especially on overnight trips, but makes for a lot of shivering during rest-stops.

The best solution for most circumstances is to wear wool clothing (trousers and shirt) which provides warmth even when wet.

The need for plenty of warm clothing when hiking above treeline cannot be stressed too much. There have been more fatalities in the Park from exposure leading to hypothermia (sub-normal body temperature) than from climbing accidents. Wind and wet weather on simple and easy trails have killed more people than icefalls.

A study by the U.S. Army Surgeon General shows a wind speed of 15 miles per hour and a temperature of 67° (which should be considered fairly "balmy" conditions in Mount Rainier meadows) are as chilling as a still-air temperature of 23°. Even in mid-summer, Mount Rainier hikers often encounter 35-mile winds and 39° temperatures—the "chill equivalent" of a still-air −38°. The combination of wind and rain or snow is even more lethal.

Hypothermia is insidious in the way it creeps up unrecognized; experienced mountaineers are caught almost as often as beginners. By the time a person realizes he is not merely weary, shivering, sluggish, and awkward of body and mind, but is suffering from hypothermia, he may have no strength left to save himself. Indeed, the mind typically becomes too dulled to be aware of danger. The victim sinks to the ground to rest "for just a minute" and slips unaware into a final sleep.

The lesson is obvious: a person who lacks sufficient clothing, shelter, and food should start for safety at first hint of bad weather—going back to the car, or at least down to timberline.

Other Equipment

Proper boots and clothing, plus perhaps a sandwich or candy bar stuffed in the pocket, suffice for the shorter and easier Mount Rainier hikes. The longer and more complicated trips demand the fuller outfit discussed in **Mountaineering: The Freedom of the Hills** (see "Recommended Reading").

From years of experience, some of it tragic, The Mountaineers have developed a list of items that should be carried by every person on any extended walk—items which provide the minimum conditions for survival when an accident or loss of route or sudden storm makes the trip longer or more severe than expected. Every person should carry these **Ten Essentials**—some in the pockets, others in the rucksack.

1. Extra clothing
2. Extra food. (The test: is there something left over at the end of the trip?)
3. Sunglasses. (Without them even a short snow crossing can be uncomfortable; prolonged snow travel can damage the eyes.)
4. Knife. (A simple pocket variety is enough; uses include first aid and emergency fire-building.)
5. Matches. (Waterproof or in a waterproof container.)

6. Firestarter. (Chemical fuels, easy burning, for starting an emergency fire with wet wood.)
7. First-aid kit
8. Flashlight
9. Map
10. Compass

Camping and Fires

Camping is the most damaging of all uses of fragile alpine meadows and if not carefully controlled quickly turns them into dustbowls.

To preserve highland gardens the Park Service has initiated a backcountry use-permit system. The system will require trial and error to perfect, but in general involves shifting most campsites from alpine meadows to wooded areas that can better withstand the impact. There will be plenty of camps for all, but at any given time a person may not be able to get his first choice of location. Reservations for specific camps may be made up to 90 days in advance; however, the hiker must claim his reservation at the Park entrance by a designated hour or lose it to someone else. In addition to permits for designated camps, a very limited number of off-trail permits are issued to give the experienced hiker a chance for solitude. Wood fires are banned at many designated camps and from all off-trail camping.

Some of the designated camps have small open-end shelter cabins. The shelters are available on a first-come first-served basis; since they hold only three or four people comfortably, most campers carry a plastic tarp or a lightweight alpine tent.

The bough bed, beloved of the frontier past, entails so much damage to vegetation that it is obsolete in many areas, including all National Parks, worthy of preservation in a natural condition. In Mount Rainier National Park, **one must never cut boughs for a bed.** Instead, carry an air mattress or a foam-plastic pad.

The wood fire, another age-old camping tradition, should also be considered obsolete in Mount Rainier high country. At best, dry firewood is hard to find at popular camps; the easy wood was burnt years ago. What remains now is largely from picturesque silver snags and down logs that are an integral part of the alpine scenery. In using such material, and even more so in cutting branches from living trees (**strictly illegal,** and they don't burn anyway) one erodes the very beauty that made the hike worth taking.

Both for reasons of convenience and scenery, The Mountaineers strongly urge alpine hikers to carry a lightweight stove for cooking and to depend on clothing and shelter (and evening strolls) for warmth. The pleasures of a roaring blaze on a cold mountain night are indisputable, but for the sake of these pleasures a single party on a single night may use up elements of the scenery that were long decades in growing, dying, and silvering.

At a few low-elevation forest camps, fires may still be built without scenic harm if a party is willing to spend time and energy ranging far through the woods looking for windfall.

Water

Hikers traditionally have drunk the water in wilderness in confidence, doing their utmost to avoid contaminating it so the next person also can safely drink. But there is no assurance your predecessor has been so careful.

No open water ever, nowadays, can be considered safe for human consumption. Any reference in this book to "drinking water" is not a guarantee. It is entirely up to the individual whether he wants to take a chance—or to treat the water with chemicals or boil it for 20 minutes.

Cross-country Hiking

Much of the Park backcountry is trail-less, kept that way to preserve some areas in as natural a condition as possible. When following a maintained trail a hiker must stick to the path to avoid extending the area of boot damage, which is particularly serious in fragile alpine plant communities. He should walk on the trail, not beside it. He should not cut switchbacks. When the tread is snowcovered, he should walk on the snow rather than detouring through meadows.

Cross-country camping is allowed for parties which have obtained the necessary permits, which are issued for groups only of five or fewer members. However, cross-country hikers must take special care not to leave marks of their passing. Following are some of the techniques by which one can minimize his impact:

Do not hike where others have. Spread out instead of going single file. Too many boots crushing plants cause erosion and new trails.

Follow the gentlest slope when ascending or descending to keep boots from digging in, crushing plants and disturbing the soil. Where possible hike on rock, snow, or through forest.

Camp in timber or rocky areas rather than on meadows. Do not camp where others have. Remove every vestige of your stay.

Enjoy wildlife from a distance, foregoing close-up photos, in order not to cause animals and birds to alter their natural habits.

Do not mark your way with cairns, flags, or other markers which encourage others to follow your footsteps. Navigate with map and compass.

Make your toilet away from watercourses. Dig a small hole about 3-6 inches deep in organic material (the biological disposer level) and replace soil when finished. Use snow, dead vegetation, or biodegradable paper.

Use tents and clothing that blend into the landscape. Avoid loud noises. Let others enjoy the solitude unaware of your presence.

Litter and Garbage

Ours is a throwaway civilization, but it is bad wildland manners to leave litter for someone else to worry about, especially in a National Park. The rule among thoughtful hikers is: **If you can carry it in full, you can carry it out empty.**

Other actions should be self-evident matters of ecological courtesy:

On a day hike, take back to the road (and garbage can) every last orange peel and gum-wrapper.

On an overnight hike burn all paper (if a fire is built) but carry back all unburnables, including metal, plastic, glass, and paper that won't burn.

Don't bury garbage. If fresh, animals will dig it up and scatter the remnants. Burning before burying is no answer either; the Park is not large enough to hide underground all the cans and bottles and debris. Tin cans may take more than 80 years to disappear completely; aluminum and glass last for centuries. Further, digging pits to

Black bear near Paradise Ranger Station

bury junk disturbs the ground cover, and iron often leaches from buried cans and "rusts" springs and creeks.

Don't leave left-over food for the next travelers; they will have their own food and won't be tempted by contributions spoiled by time or chewed by animals.

Especially don't cache plastic tarps. Weathering quickly ruins the fabric, little creatures nibble, and the result is a useless, miserable mess.

Bears

If every hiker were to scrupulously avoid advertising himself as proprietor of a traveling supermarket, the "bear problem" would completely disappear in a very few years, the animals quickly reverting to their natural foods. This must become every hiker's goal.

The problem cannot be solved by merely hanging food bags from trees. Bears which develop a dependence on man's bounty quickly learn to climb the tree and make a flying leap for the bag. It is necessary for all—not just some—hikers to conspire to keep from bears the secret that backpackers carry eatables. This may be done by:

Never leaving a scrap of garbage, not even cracker crumbs "for the chipmunks." Never tossing bacon grease or fish guts or the like in the bushes. **Pack it out.**

Always keeping food in tight containers to prevent aromas from spreading on the breezes. Always keeping these containers in a tough food bag in a closed pack near the party. The tree-hanging method of storage is good, but only if the hikers are around to repel raids with loud noises. If allowed sufficient time, a hungry bear always will gain access to an untended cache.

Theft

Twenty years ago theft from a car left at a forest or National Park trailhead was rare. Not now. Equipment has become so fancy and expensive, so much worth stealing, and hikers so numerous, their throngs creating large assemblages of valuables, that theft is a growing problem. Not even wilderness camps are entirely safe; a single raider hitting an unguarded camp may easily carry off several sleeping bags, a couple of tents, and assorted stoves, down booties, and freeze-dried strawberries—maybe $1000 worth of gear in one load! However, the professionals who do most of the stealing mainly concentrate on cars. Authorities are concerned but can't post guards at every trailhead.

National Park rangers have the following recommendations:

First and foremost don't make crime profitable for the pros. If they break into a hundred cars and get nothing but moldy boots and tattered T-shirts they'll give up. The best bet is to arrive in a beat-up 1960 car with doors and windows that don't close and leave in it nothing of value. If you insist on driving a nice new car, at least don't have mag wheels, tape deck, and radio, and keep it empty of gear. Don't think locks help—pros can open your car door and trunk as fast with a picklock as you can with your key. Don't imagine you can hide anything from them—they know all the hiding spots. If the hike is part of an extended car trip, arrange to store your extra equipment at a nearby motel.

Be suspicious of anyone waiting at a trailhead. One of the tricks of the trade is to sit there with a pack as if waiting for a ride, watching new arrivals unpack—and hide their valuables—and maybe even striking up a conversation to determine how long the marks will be away.

The ultimate solution, of course, is for hikers to become as poor as they were in the olden days. No criminal would consider trailheads profitable if the loot consisted solely of shabby khaki war surplus.

Climbing Mount Rainier

The summit of Mount Rainier has an irresistible attraction, and each year about 7000 people start for the summit; some 4000 succeed. The only basic requirements are good physical condition and stubborn determination. Those under 19 years of age must carry written permission of a parent or guardian.

The popular climbing season is from the second weekend in May through the second weekend in September.

Before trying for the summit, check with your physician, then get into top condition by taking strenuous hikes every weekend and jogging several miles each day. Take every opportunity to walk or run instead of riding.

There are two ways to prepare for a climb. The best is to enroll in a climbing school offered by a mountaineering club, master the fundamentals of the sport on lesser peaks, and come to Mount Rainier fully qualified to tackle it. Experienced climbers can obtain permission for the ascent upon request. Parties should consist of three or more members.

A second way is to join a professionally guided party at Paradise. The guide service is used by novices and good climbers short of knowledge of glacier travel and crevasse rescue. The inexperienced climber must first spend a day at the guide-operated school learning crevasse rescue and use of ice ax and rope. Guides furnish their clients the necessary equipment. Full information can be obtained by writing the Superintendent, Mount Rainier National Park, Ashford, Washington 98304. Phone Area Code 206 569-2211.

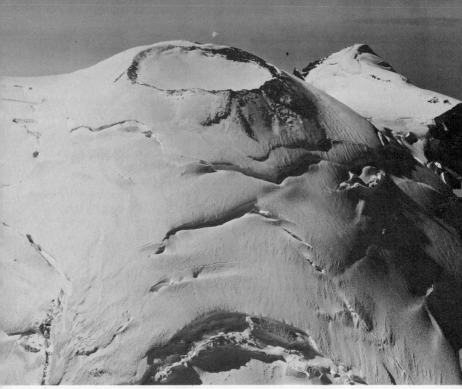

Air view of the crater on Columbia Crest, Liberty Cap to the right. Notice the difficulty of crossing the top bergschrund

Unguided parties must register and obtain a backcountry use permit at Park headquarters or any ranger station. This can be done any day from 8 to 5, or other hours by arrangement with the area rangers. Phone 206-569-2211.

The following personal equipment is needed: climbing boots, full-frame steel crampons (that fit), ice ax, three prusik slings, adequate inner and outer clothing, mittens, sunglasses or goggles, sun cream, first aid kit, food, and sleeping bag. The following party equipment is required: climbing rope equal to or better than ⅜-inch synthetic fiber, a minimum of one 120-foot rope for each three persons, topographic map, compass, and flashlights or headlights. The following equipment is recommended: stove, matches, extra food and clothing, wands, water bottle, carabiners, hard hats, pulleys, and tarp or tent. Most of these items can be rented or purchased from the guide service at Paradise. At the time of check-in, rangers will provide information on current route conditions.

The two most popular routes to the summit are by way of Camp Muir-Ingraham Glacier and Camp Schurman-Emmons Glacier. Both ways require two or more days.

The first day on the Muir-Ingraham route is spent checking out and hiking from Paradise to Camp Muir (Hike 45). The climb begins between 1 and 3 the following morning, to take advantage of firm snow that turns to mush under the afternoon sun. The route generally crosses the Cowlitz Glacier and climbs beside the Ingraham Glacier to the top, but the way changes from week to week as crevasses open and ice bridges break. Allow 6 to 8 hours from Camp Muir to the summit, and 2 to 3 hours to descend. Over 300 people have been counted at Camp Muir on a single night, terrifically overloading sanitary facilities. But more important, there is a physical restriction on how many climbers can pass Cowlitz Cleaver at a time; some climbers have had to wait 1½ hours for their turn. For this reason a limit is imposed on the number of climbers using a given route at any one time.

The Schurman-Emmons route is generally easier. However, the starting point is much lower and the hiking distance considerably longer. For this reason many prefer to spend 2½ days. From the White River Campground, follow the trail to Glacier Basin (Hike 21) and perhaps the first night's camp. Leave trail and climb Interglacier to Steamboat Prow and high camp near Schurman Hut (an emergency cabin). The departure time next morning is between midnight and 4. The route varies considerably during the summer but generally follows "The Corridor," a relatively smooth snow ridge dividing the Emmons and Winthrop Glaciers. The biggest problem is often finding a route around or over the big bergschrund near the top. Some years there isn't any easy way.

This Land is Your Land

Some of the above paragraphs may strike a hiker raised in the frontier tradition as being too heavy on "don'ts." However, neither The Mountaineers nor the National Park Service seek to restrict freedom of enjoyment. Rather, the intent is to suggest how one may enjoy the Park without destroying the pleasure of others who will follow the same trails tomorrow, next summer, and in years to come.

Mount Rainier National Park is the property of every American. For each of us and all of us, it is home, if we make it so, and treat it so.

THE MOUNTAINEERS:
AN INVITATION

The Mountaineers, with groups based in Seattle, Everett, Tacoma, and Olympia, warmly invite the membership of all lovers of outdoor life who sympathize with the purposes of the organization and wish to share its activities.

The Mountaineers sponsor a year-around program of climbing, hiking, camping, ski-touring, and snowshoeing. Many hundreds of outings are scheduled each year, ranging from afternoon walks to trips lasting 2 weeks or more. On a typical weekend as many as 50 excursions may be offered, from ocean beaches to the summit of Mount Rainier. In addition, members engage in countless privately-organized trips of all kinds; the opportunity is boundless to make new friends with similar interests.

Enjoying wildlands is one side of the coin; the other is working to preserve the natural beauty of Northwest America. Here, The Mountaineers continue their role of leadership as they have for more than 70 years.

For a membership application, and further information on club activities, write The Mountaineers, 719 Pike Street, Seattle, Washington 98101.

EXPLANATION OF SYMBOLS

 Easy strolls. No special clothing or equipment required. Hikes which can be accomplished by nearly everybody in a day or less.

 Hikes requiring at least a minimum of equipment — lug-soled boots, sturdy clothing, rucksack with the 10 Essentials. (See page 8.)

 Hikes especially suited for overnight trips. Although most of the hikes in this book can be completed round trip in one day by a strong hiker carrying only a light rucksack, these trips are recommended for overnight outings.

 Carry water. Water may not be available or may be unsafe for drinking.

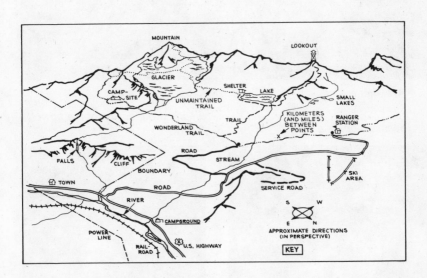

Avalanche lilies

False Solomon's seal

Elephant head, one of the figwort family

Bear grass

Raccoons at Longmire Campground

Cascades golden-mantled ground squirrel

Clark's nutcracker

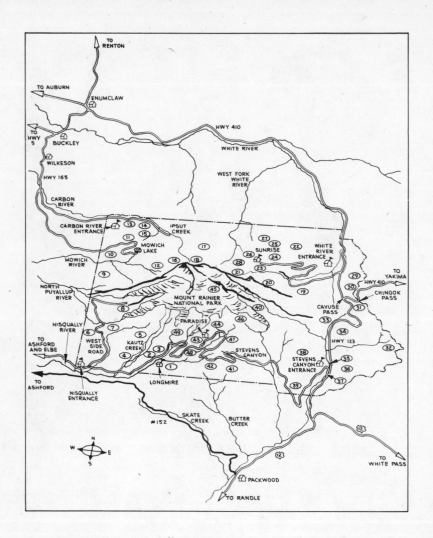

50 HIKES IN
MOUNT RAINIER NATIONAL PARK

1 Eagle Peak Saddle

Round trip 11km (7 miles)
Hiking time 5 hours
High point 1720 meters (5650 feet)
Elevation gain 900 meters (2955 feet)
Snowfree July
to October

A forest hike to a great view of Mount Rainier from a high saddle on the west end of the Tatoosh Range.

Drive from National Park Inn at Longmire past the Ranger Station and residences, cross the suspension bridge over the Nisqually River, and park in front of the community house. Walk back up the road toward the bridge. Sometimes the road is closed, in which case park in the Longmire parking area. Cross the bridge and continue 60 meters (200 feet) to trailhead on the left.

Most of the hike lies in virgin forest on a wide, smooth path with an easy grade. The first 1½km (mile) is an aisle through a dense undercover of salal. Around 3km (2 miles) is a small stream, the last water. At about 5km (3¼ miles), good trail ends below a high-angle meadow, which in late June explodes with flowers, the Tatoosh Range adding an inspiring backdrop for the fields of bear grass. A final steep and rocky ¾km (½ mile) climbs to the 1720-meter (5700-foot) saddle, where all semblance of trail disappears.

Walk a short way to the right for the best view of Mount Rainier. East is the Tatoosh Range. West and down is Longmire. South rise Adams and St. Helens, beyond miles and miles of private tree farms and the Gifford Pinchot National Forest. Eagle Peak is very close to the Park boundary, providing a good opportunity to see the difference between multiple-used lands and a "museum of primitive America." Essential as logging is to the economy, the contrast makes one thankful that some samples of natural forest are being saved within National Parks.

The saddle is the essential turnaround point for hikers; the final 100 meters (300 feet) to the summit of Eagle Peak is strictly for trained climbers. Climbers consider the summit ascent easy enough; the rock is solid and the ledge wide. However, the danger of a fall is great. In any event, the view from the saddle is just as good as that from the top.

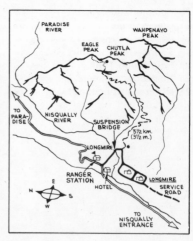

Cloud-shrouded Eagle Peak

The climbing route goes up a rocky rib from the saddle toward the peak, then traverses through a thicket on the left slope. At one point the best way seems to be a switchback under a 10-meter (30-foot) cliff—which, however, leads to the edge of nothing. The proper way drops **under** the cliff and then climbs back up and traverses across the face of the cliff on a "broad" 1-meter (3-foot) ledge. The rock is sound, with numerous holds, but slippery when wet. Novices tempted to try it should remember that going down is many times harder than going up.

LONGMIRE

2 Trail Of The Shadows

Loop trip 1km (¾ mile)
Hiking time 30 minutes
Snowfree ⅔
   of the year

The Trail of the Shadows is a self-guiding nature walk past mineral springs, a cabin built in 1888, and through a lovely cool forest.

Drive from the Nisqually Entrance 9½km (6 miles) to Longmire. Trail begins directly across highway from the hotel. Outstanding features are numbered and keyed to a booklet, copies of which may be picked up at the start of the trail. To follow the booklet, go counterclockwise on the loop trail.

The center of the loop is mostly open marshy meadow with active beaver dams and numerous mineral springs, some slightly warm; the trail passes near two of them. James Longmire, on a trip to Paradise, discovered the springs, which then were considerably warmer than now. In 1884 he staked a mineral claim and established a hotel. The existing cabin was built by his son in 1888 on a homestead claim.

Homestead cabin on Trail of the Shadows

The trail continues past the cabin into dense forest. Three-fourths of the way around is the junction with the trail which from here climbs over Rampart Ridge (Hike 3).

Lovely in all seasons, in October the trail gives its final color show before the snows, a display of the strikingly-beautiful, but deadly, gold-and-orange amanita mushrooms. Remember: for all to enjoy, nothing should be removed.

Three woods walks in the Longmire area are worth the hour or less of easy strolling they require:

Cougar Rock to Longmire

From the entrance to Cougar Rock Campground, cross the highway and walk down the shoulder to the first curve. Find the trail near a service road. The way passes through a pleasant forest between the highway and the Nisqually River, sometimes in sight of the river. One-way distance 3km (2 miles), all downhill.

Nisqually River Trails

West side. From Longmire go toward the old Longmire Campground. Just short of the suspension bridge find the trail on the left, near the cable anchors. The path follows the river through forest ¾km (½ mile) to a junction with the Wonderland Trail.

East side. Cross the suspension bridge and find the trail on the upstream side near the cable anchors. The path goes ¾km (½ mile) along the stream before ending.

Twin Firs Loop Trail

A grove of large trees and nurse logs, a fine example of a climax forest, on a short ¾km (½-mile) loop. However, finding the trail is very tricky. Drive exactly 1.5km (.9 mile) toward Longmire from the Kautz Creek bridge or 3.4km (2.1 miles) from Longmire toward the Nisqually Entrance to a small paved parking area on the north side of the road. At the lower end are twin firs, two large trees growing side by side. One of the trees has lost its top.

The trail (unmarked) starts behind the twin firs, parallels the road a few feet, climbs uphill, bridging several small streams, and then descends and ends within a few feet of the parking area. The hike can be done in either direction, but there is a confusion of trails at the start if hiked in reverse.

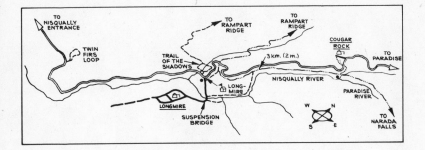

Tumtum Peak from Rampart Ridge trail

LONGMIRE

3 Rampart Ridge

Loop trip 7¼km (4.5 miles)
Hiking time 2½ hours
High point 1244 meters (4080 feet)
Elevation gain 550 meters (1800 feet)
Snowfree mid-June
to October

A loop trip through fine forests, climbing to a cliff-edge panorama of the Nisqually River valley. The trail is in excellent condition, but carry water. There is none on the way.

Drive to Longmire, where the hike begins and ends. It doesn't really matter which direction is taken, but by going clockwise one has glimpses of the mountain while walking along the ridge.

Find the Trail of the Shadows nature walk directly across the road from the National Park Inn. Take the **left** (reverse) segment of the loop 250 meters (800 feet) to a junction with the Rampart Ridge trail.

The wide path ascends through woods 3km (2 miles), in a series of long switchbacks, to the ridge crest. The last switchback gives an interesting view of Tumtum Peak to the west. Then comes a cliff-top overlook of Longmire and the entire Nisqually River valley, all the way up to the buildings at Paradise.

Shortly beyond, the trail levels into a flat mile along the ridge. At the junction with the Wonderland Trail, go right. In a bit is another junction, this time with a trail to Van Trump Park; again go right, dropping into the valley. Just before reaching Longmire the trail crosses the road; pick it up again on the far side and return to the parking lot.

Those who want views will find excellent vistas on the ridge.

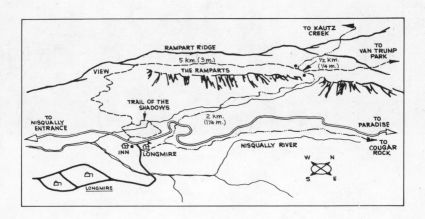

Mount Rainier from Kautz Creek

4 Kautz Creek

Round trip 17½km (11 miles)
Hiking time 6 hours
High point 1710 meters (5600 feet)
Elevation gain 700 meters (2300 feet)
Snowfree mid-July
to mid-October

A trail with a long history, being the earliest way used to reach Indian Henrys Hunting Ground. Begins in the Kautz Creek flood area and passes through forest to the high meadow country.

Hikers on their first trip to Indian Henrys will want to save time and energy for explorations when they get there, and therefore should take the shorter route up Tahoma Creek (Hike 5). However, though 3km (2 miles) longer, the Kautz trail is the more interesting, giving an unusual perspective of the mountain. If doing the hike early in the summer, make sure before starting that the footbridge is in place over the creek; high water frequently washes it away.

Drive from the Nisqually Entrance 5km (3 miles) toward Longmire and park by the nature exhibit at the Kautz Creek bridge. The trail starts on the opposite side of the highway.

The trail winds a short and easy way along the smooth top of the Kautz Mudflow, crosses Kautz Creek, and immediately enters virgin forest. The next stretch is a gentle climb, followed by a steep series of switchbacks pulling out of the valley.

In about 6½km (4 miles) the trail moderates a bit and enters meadows with views south and west. Farther along, Point Success, the second-highest of Mount Rainier's three summits, can be seen poking over the ridge ahead. Early in the season there is some very muddy tread on a steep hillside. Finally the grade levels and the last 1km (¾ mile) traverses around the flank of Mt. Ararat and drops down to Indian Henrys. (Mt. Ararat was named by Ben Longmire, who claimed to have found on this peak some petrified planks and a petrified stump with what appeared to be an old cable scar around it. Thus, this must have been where Noah's ark first touched land.)

Exploring at Indian Henrys is described in Hike 5.

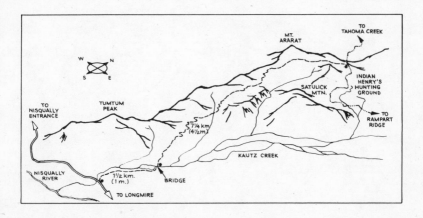

WEST SIDE ROAD

5 Indian Henrys Hunting Ground

Round trip from Tahoma Creek 11km (7 miles)
Hiking time 4 hours
High point 1675 meters (5500 feet)
Elevation gain 760 meters (2500 feet)
Snowfree mid-July
    to mid-October

Hike through splendid forest to one of the Park's loveliest alpine meadows and probably the most famous single view of the mountain.

Drive a short 1½km (1 mile) from the Nisqually Entrance and turn left on the West Side Road 7¼km (4½ miles) to the Tahoma Creek Picnic Area. Trail begins at the upper end.

The way first passes through the blowdown of October 1962, which flattened 2.75 hectare (6.75 acres) of trees. Next comes a steady climb, usually within sight of Tahoma Creek, to a junction with the Wonderland Trail at 3km (2 miles). The left fork goes to Emerald Ridge (Hike 7). Take the right fork, crossing Tahoma Creek; just beyond is a striking look upward to Glacier Island, which very recently was literally an island between two rivers of ice. Ascending through forest, at 5½km (3½ miles) the trail emerges into Indian Henrys Hunting Ground. Some 300-500 people visit Indian Henrys on a summer day. To protect the fragile meadow from this heavy use, camping has been moved 1km (¾ mile) toward Kautz Creek near Devils Dream Creek. The Ranger Station is near the junction of the Kautz Creek trail.

The famous view—portrayed on a commemorative postage stamp in 1934—is from Mirror Lake, reached via a 1km (¾-mile) spur trail starting in the first meadow and wandering amid flowers toward the mountain. For those staying overnight: rise in early morning and climb to the top of Pyramid Peak, a steep but short and easy ascent; at the summit, confronted by The Mountain, one will know the meaning of insignificance.

If transportation can be arranged, a 14½km (9-mile) straight-through hike can be made from Tahoma Creek to the Kautz Mudflow (Hike 4). Even more interesting is to follow the Wonderland Trail 10½km (6½ miles) down from Indian Henrys to Longmire 16km (10 miles total from Tahoma Creek). The route passes swampy Squaw Lake, goes along the edge of Devils Canyon, a deep cleft hidden in forest, drops into the hole dug by the Kautz Flood, climbs 120 meters (400 feet) onto Rampart Ridge, and descends to Longmire (Hike 3).

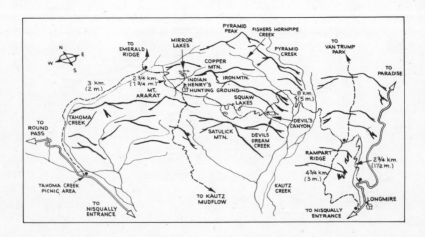

Mirror Lake and Mount Rainier taken from the same place as Asahel Curtis's famous picture

WEST SIDE ROAD

6 Gobblers Knob

To Lake George:
   Round trip 3km (2 miles)
   Hiking time 1½ hours
   High point 1290 meters (4232 feet)
   Elevation gain 70 meters (232 feet)
   Snowfree June
      through October

To Gobblers Knob:
   Round trip 8km (5 miles)
   Hiking time 3 hours
   High point 1675 meters (5500 feet)
   Elevation gain 460 meters (1500 feet)
   Snowfree July
      to mid-October

A wide, well-beaten path to a mountain lake tucked away in forest and to a fire lookout with a grand view of Tahoma Glacier and Sunset Amphitheater.

Drive a short 1½km (1 mile) from the Nisqually Entrance to the West Side Road and turn left 11km (7 miles) to Round Pass. Trail begins from parking lot at the left of the road.

The smooth trail, probably the most popular on the west side of the mountain, gains elevation steadily but easily, reaching Lake George in a bit less than 1½km (1 mile). The lake, almost ¾km (½ mile) long, is a popular campsite both for fishermen and beginning hikers on their first backpack. There is a shelter—usually full. A way trail goes around the righthand shore, to views of Mount Rainier. The left shore has too many steep cliffs for a decent passage.

The trail climbs a somewhat steeper but still quite gentle 2½km (1½ miles) from the lake to Gobblers Knob, the most northerly bump on the long ridge of Mt. Wow. A short distance below the top, a 2½km (1½-mile) side-trail drops to Goat Lake, outside the Park; camping at Goat Lake is more private than at Lake George. Beyond the junction

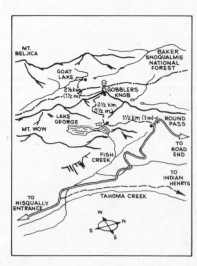

Alpine fir tree on side of Gobblers Knob

Mount Rainier from Gobblers Knob

the way emerges from forest to the odd and striking cliffs of the Knob, a rock garden of juniper, red heather, phlox, and other flowers in season.

The horizon from the lookout cabin is all Mount Rainier on one side—but on others, St. Helens, Adams, Hood, and the Olympic Mountains. A substantial reward for a leisurely afternoon.

7 Emerald Ridge

Round trip 11km (7 miles)
Hiking time 5 hours
High point 1705 meters (5600 feet)
Elevation gain 610 meters (2000 feet)
Snowfree July
to mid-October

Take a little-used access to the Wonderland Trail and then climb beside the Tahoma Glacier to an emerald-green ridge with a close-up look at living ice and an unusual view of the mountain.

Drive a short 1½km (1 mile) from the Nisqually Entrance to the West Side Road and turn left 12km (7.5 miles), crossing Round Pass and continuing to the trailhead (South Fork trail), shortly before the crossing of the South Fork Puyallup River.

The trail passes through a deep forest, including giant cedars. In 3km (2 miles) look for tall colonnades of columnar andesite, one of the finest examples in the Park. The columns (usually hexagonal) were formed when hot lava flowed into the valley; the pattern developed as a result of shrinkage during cooling. Shortly beyond is the junction with the Wonderland Trail. The left fork crosses the river and ascends to St. Andrews Park and Klapatche Park. Small campsite here.

The right fork climbs to the ridge in about 3km (2 miles), following old moraines and riverbeds full of cobblestones, becoming steeper, but still easy enough going. Note the variety of evergreen and deciduous trees reforesting the morainal debris. As elevation is gained the Tahoma Glacier comes in sight, its flow split by Emerald Ridge into two tongues, the northeast lobe providing the source of the South Puyallup River.

The ridge top is a small, open, very green meadow, though with few flowers. Watch for goats. The "prow" of the ridge offers a splendid view up the glacier to Tokaloo Rock and the Puyallup Cleaver. To the right is the prominent cliff of Glacier Island, which until 40 years ago was completely surrounded by ice; now only barren moraines are left at its base.

If transportation can be arranged, continue around the ridge and descend to the Tahoma Creek trail and out to the West Side Road—a route only ¾km (½ mile) longer than the way in and with a slightly better path.

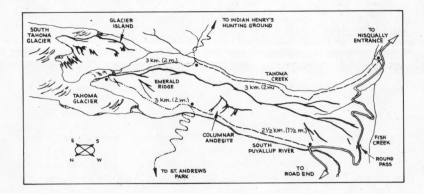

Emerald Ridge and Glacier Island

The Colonnades

WEST SIDE ROAD

8 Klapatche Park

Round trip to Klapatche 8km (5 miles)
Hiking time 3-4 hours
High point 1675 meters (5500 feet)
Elevation gain 520 meters (1700 feet)
Snowfree mid-July
    to mid-October

An all-time favorite camp near a small mountain lake surrounded by green meadows. Magnificent view of Sunset Amphitheater, and a dramatic place to watch the sunset. Klapatche can be reached by either of two ways, both easy—but one easier, and the other more scenic.

For the easiest route, drive a short 1½km (1 mile) from the Nisqually Entrance and turn left on the West Side Road. At 17½km (11 miles) cross St. Andrews Creek and park. An interesting 20-minute side-trip is the St. Andrews Creek trail which leads down through cool forest ⅓km (¼ mile) to Denman Falls. The Klapatche Ridge trail starts 30 meters (100 feet) beyond the bridge. The wide, smooth way climbs steadily through forest to the ridge crest, which it then follows to a surprisingly abrupt opening into the meadows at 4km (2½ miles).

For the more rugged route, continue on the West Side Road 6½km (4 miles) beyond St. Andrews Creek to the road-end at the North Puyallup River. The trail, part of the Wonderland Trail, starts on the uphill side of the large parking lot. This way is ⅓km (¼ mile) longer than the other, starts 100 meters (300 feet) lower, and is not so well-kept, but the last ¾km (½ mile) gives a unique view of the mountain that makes the extra effort worthwhile.

The trails enter the large 1675-meter (5500-foot) meadow from opposite directions. Aurora Lake lies on the south side, a marvelous reflecting mirror for the mountain. West of the lake, tucked in the trees, are a few campsites. A water well is located a few hundred feet north of the lake. No wood fires.

The side-trip to St. Andrews Park is mandatory. Follow the Wonderland Trail 1km (¾ mile) through flower gardens, past a grand overlook of the mountain, to 1830-meter (6000-foot) St. Andrews Lake. Wander the heather benches and creeks of the park. The lake usually doesn't melt completely free of ice until August.

Hikers with an extra couple of hours available won't want to stop here. From the lake scramble up meadows and scree (avoiding steep snowfields) to the ridge and wander on and on by ponds, through tiny flower gardens, above moraines, toward Tokaloo Rock. The end of easy travel is at about 2100 meters (7000 feet), an hour above St. Andrews. The Tahoma Glacier, sweeping down from the summit icecap, dominates the ridge-roaming walk.

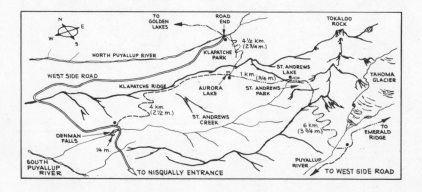

Aurora Lake and Mount Rainier from Klapatche Park   37

9 Golden Lakes and Sunset Lookout

Round trip 15km (9½ miles)
Hiking time 6 hours
High point 1688 meters (5537 feet)
Elevation gain 620 meters (2037 feet)
Snowfree July
to mid-October

A ghostly silver forest, alpine meadows scattered with Golden Lakes, and a side-trip to a lookout with supreme views of the mountain and the Puget Sound country.

Drive a short 1½km (mile) from the Nisqually Entrance to the West Side Road and turn left 24km (15 miles) to the road-end at the North Puyallup River. Trail begins to the left of the parking lot.

The walk begins with an ideal warm-up section, dropping a few meters after crossing the river, then going almost level for the first 1½km (mile); when climbing does begin, it's almost too gradual to be noticed. Eventually, though, the way becomes perceptibly steep, climbing out of the valley and emerging from forest into the weather-bleached snags of the silver forest. (These trees were killed in early November 1930 by a runaway fire started by contractors engaged in clearing operations for a proposed extension of the West Side Road.) Some years the area displays an immense field of bear grass blossoms.

At 5½km (3½ miles) is Sunset Park and a junction. The left fork goes 2km (1¼ miles) to the camping area and Golden Lakes. The largest lake is ¾km (½ mile) beyond, hidden in trees about 150 meters (500 feet) below the trail. One must look carefully and perhaps use a contour map to find it, or settle for the smaller and higher lakes.

If views are the aim, take the right fork from Sunset Park junction to Lookout Point. The climb is easy through open meadows which seem to lead directly into the mountain. Fine vistas here of Sunset Amphitheater and ice cliffs on Ptarmigan Ridge. From here one can see down into the Golden Lakes. As the name implies, this is a spectacular place to watch the sunset—and afterward, the lights of Puget Sound cities. If camping, carry a stove; wood fires are not allowed.

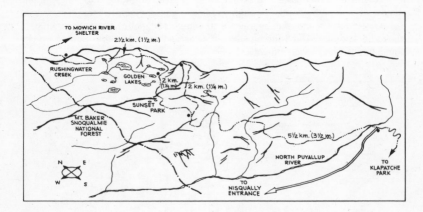

Mount Rainier and The Colonnade from trail to Golden Lakes

MOWICH LAKE AND
CARBON RIVER

10 Paul Peak Loop

Round trip (to Mowich River Shelter) 12km (7½ miles)
Loop trip 18½km (11½ miles)
Hiking time 3 hours
High point 1035 meters (3400 feet)
Elevation gain 250 meters (800 feet)
Snowfree April or
May through October

An easy walk through deep timber, ideal for spring and autumn hiking when higher trails are under snow. Short on broad vistas, but long on the quiet intimacy of virgin forest, ethereal in fall mists. Look for mushrooms beside the trail.

Drive the Mowich Entrance road to the Paul Peak picnic area ¾km (½ mile) inside the Park boundary. The trail leaves the right side of the picnic area, drops gradually downhill, rounds Paul Peak, and at 5½km (3½ miles) joins the Wonderland Trail. Take the right fork, crossing a log bridge to three shelters located between the North and South Mowich Rivers. This side of the mountain has few visitors, so the shelters are often empty. Water available from the river. Driftwood along the river banks may seem wet but burns well.

During summer months a loop trip can be made by way of Mowich Lake. Recross the North Mowich River and follow the Wonderland Trail. From the river the trail becomes a series of switchbacks climbing 600 meters (2000 feet) in 3km (2 miles), then leveling into a gently-climbing 1½km (mile) along Crater Creek to Mowich Lake and the road-end.

Rather than walk the road back to the start, at the lake find the historic Grindstone Trail, completed by Bailey Willis in 1884 and recently re-opened. To shortcut the long switchbacks of the road, follow it 6km (3¾ miles) down to the start, for a total round-trip hike of 17½km (11 miles).

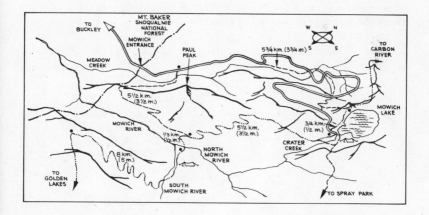

Twin-flower growing near the Mowich River trail

MOWICH LAKE AND CARBON RIVER

11 Tolmie Peak

Round trip 10½km (6½ miles)
Hiking time 3 hours
High point 1810 meters (5939 feet)
Elevation gain 308 meters (1010 feet)
Snowfree mid-July
    through September

A view supreme and a serene alpine lake. This is the peak long thought to have been climbed in 1833 by Dr. Tolmie, first white man to visit what is now the Park. (Recent research indicates Tolmie actually climbed Hessong Rock, closer to the mountain.)

Drive via Buckley and Wilkerson to the Mowich Entrance and continue to road-end at Mowich Lake. The way is generally rough, but passable at slow speeds. Before reaching the Park one can enjoy (if that is the word) an enormous panorama of clearcut logging from the valleys up onto the slopes of the mountain itself.

Find the trail on the left side of the road just on arriving at the lake. The path skirts the forested shores on a fairly level grade, rising and falling a bit. At 2km (1¼ miles) is Ipsut Pass, where the Wonderland Trail descends right 6½km (4 miles) to the Carbon River (Hike 15). Take the left fork another 1½ km (1 mile) to Eunice Lake, first dropping 30 meters (100 feet), then in the final ¾km (½ mile) turning steeply up.

Eunice Lake, at an elevation of 1632 meters (5355 feet), is one of the prettiest in the Park. Rising above is Tolmie Peak, the lookout cabin plainly visible. Follow the trail around the left shore and see Mount Rainier across the foreground of wind-rippling, sun-sparkling water.

Explore the meadows around the lake. Though these are not the vast flower fields of Spray Park or Paradise, many varieties can be found here, as well as extensive evidence of Rainier's volcanic origin.

But the trip is incomplete without climbing the steep but short 1½km (1 mile) to the lookout. South is Mt. St. Helens, west the Olympics, and north Mt. Baker. Directly below on one side is Green Lake (Hike 14), and on the other Eunice Lake, and off where the hike began, Mowich Lake. North is the immense logging scar on Cayada Creek. Southeast, of course, is The Mountain.

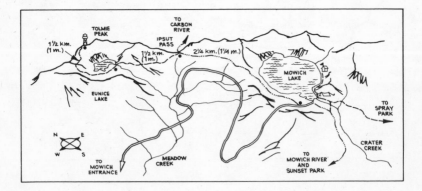

Eunice Lake and Mount Rainier from trail to Tolmie Peak   43

MOWICH LAKE AND CARBON RIVER

12 Spray Park

Round trip (to the broad meadow under Mt. Pleasant) about 9½km (6 miles)
Hiking time 3 hours
High point 1770 meters (5800 feet)
Elevation gain 320 meters (1050 feet)
Snowfree mid-July
  through October

Every Rainier hiker has his favorite, but many argue this is the supreme flower garden in the Park. Pond-sprinkled meadows, easy-roaming ridges, endless and delightful nooks and crannies. In the past as many as 185 campers were counted at Spray Park, with another 200 day hikers. To let the meadows recover from years of such impact, camping is now prohibited. However, camping is allowed at Mowich Lake and Eagle Roost Camp near Spray Falls.

Drive via Buckley and Wilkerson to the Mowich Entrance and continue to the road-end at Mowich Lake.

Find the trail at the large parking lot on the west side of the lake. The path drops a bit, coming in less than ¹/₃km (¼ mile) to the junction with the Sunset Park trail. Go left, contouring through subalpine forest, up a little, down a little, around the side of Fay Peak and Hessong Rock. At 2½km (1½ miles) is Eagle Cliff, a good place to rest and look at the mountain, including a portion of the Mowich Glacier. At 3km (2 miles) a side-trail crosses a footlog and goes ¹/₃km (¼ mile) to Spray Falls, a wide splash of water; only a fraction of the falls can be seen—the main part is uphill, out of sight—but what can be seen is beautiful enough.

From the falls the trail switchbacks steeply up some 200 meters (600 feet) in ¾km (½ mile) to the lowermost meadows of Spray Park. Day hikers often have lunch here and turn around, well-satisfied with the flowers and with the glaciers seen beyond 2377-meter (7800-foot) Echo Rock and 2530-meter (8300-foot) Observation Rock. However, the first really broad meadow, under Mt. Pleasant, is another few minutes, and the farther one goes, the better the views. A week is scarcely sufficient for all the appealing walks.

One obvious side-trip is to continue on the trail to the 1950-meter (6400-foot) ridge above Seattle Park (Hike 16); on a clear day the view from this ridge extends all the way beyond lower buttresses of Mount Rainier to the North Cascades. Another is to climb 1967-meter (6453-foot) Mt. Pleasant, appropriately named, an easy stroll up open meadows.

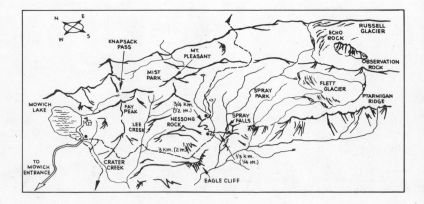

Mount Rainier and avalanche lilies in Spray Park

To fully appreciate the dimensions and magnificence of Spray Park, strike off toward the mountain, past waterfalls and ponds and ice-scratched-and-polished buttresses. Seek out the hidden, glacier-fed lake behind a moraine at the foot of Observation Rock. Wander onto the ridge overlooking the Carbon Glacier and Willis Wall.

13 Carbon River Trails

The Olympic rain forest—that's what one is reminded of when walking amid the cool, damp growth of the Carbon River valley, seeing the moss-draped trees, the soft carpet of moss on the ground, the classic examples of nurse logs, and all the thriving life in the green-gloomy understory.

Drive via Buckley and Wilkerson to the Carbon River Entrance. No trail runs the length of the forest but several short spurs offer easy samples.

Rain Forest Loop Nature Trail

This is the only known inland example of temperate rain forest, which usually occurs near the ocean coast.

Find the self-guiding nature trail, with numbered steps discussing the rain-forest environment, on the right side of the road at the Park entrance. A ¾km (½-mile) loop partly through a marsh and partly through trees. At the upper end of the loop is an unmarked junction with the Boundary Trail, a seldom-maintained and seldom-used and hazardous route winding along the Park boundary toward the Mowich Entrance. (Those thinking about hiking the Boundary Trail should ask the ranger at Carbon River for the latest information. The middle ¾km (½ mile) of the route is in a clearcut outside the Park and the trail is non-existent.)

Mine Path

A short walk, several hundred feet, through mosses and nurse logs of the climax

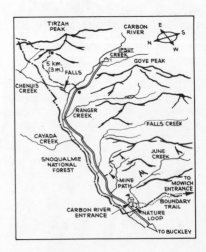

June Creek nature trail

forest. One can continue to the mine but it is boarded up and not worth a visit. Find the unmaintained and unmarked trail on the right side of the road between 1½ and 2½km (1 and 1½ miles) from the Park entrance. Space for one or two cars to park.

Chenuis Falls

Drive about 5½km (3½ miles) from the Park entrance to parking space and sign on the left. The trail crosses the Carbon River on a bridge and winds through forest a short bit to the falls, which cascade down a series of rock slabs.

Ipsut Falls Nature Trail

Drive to the road-end at Ipsut Creek Campground. A self-guiding nature trail discussing the role of water in the ecosystem goes a short way to Ipsut Falls.

MOWICH LAKE AND CARBON RIVER

14 Green Lake

Round trip 6½km (4 miles)
Hiking time 2 hours
High point 915 meters (3000 feet)
Elevation gain 305 meters (1000 feet)
Snowfree May
  to November

In a National Park with many wonderful forest trails, this easy walk to a crystal-clear lake stands far above all the rest.

Drive to the Carbon River Entrance and 4¾km (3 miles) beyond to a small parking space at Ranger Creek crossing (a culvert). Trail is on the right.

The beginning is a climb through a grove of giant trees, centuries old. During the first ¾km (½ mile) the floor is rich in ferns and devil's club. One gnarled root system would serve as a proper throne for a forest prince. Above the path are numerous tree bridges—overpasses for squirrels, no doubt.

In 1½km (1 mile) take a short side-trip to Ranger Creek Falls. In 2½km (1½ miles) the track levels and crosses the clear-watered creek, and at 3km (2 miles) reaches the lake, deep in lush forest. (Because of extreme fire hazard in the deep forest duff, and the large number of visitors who easily could "love the lake to death," camping is not permitted here.)

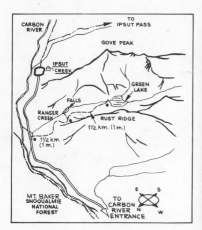

Ranger Creek trail

Ranger Creek Falls

MOWICH LAKE AND CARBON RIVER

15 Ipsut Creek

Round trip to Ipsut Pass 12¾km (8 miles)
Hiking time 4 hours
High point 1550 meters (5100 feet)
Elevation gain 800 meters (2600 feet)
Snowfree June
    through October

A forested segment of the Wonderland Trail passing the world's largest known Alaska yellow-cedar. The woods walk as far as the big tree is pleasant in itself, particularly early in the season when the high country is buried in snow.

Drive to the Carbon River Entrance and continue to the road-end at Ipsut Creek Campground. The trail starts at the upper end of the camping area, follows the dirt road 100 meters (300 feet) toward the horse corral, then turns right at a prominent sign. In a short distance climbing begins. The path is wide and mostly smooth. The trees are impressively tall, and the ground is carpeted with moss and flowers. The trail continues steadily upward, crossing numerous small streams. Ipsut Creek is a constant roar on the right.

In about 5km (3 miles) the way emerges from forest and crosses the creek, which though still noisy is now only a step wide. The specimen cedar is in a grove of alpine trees just beyond the crossing. Actually, after the huge firs and hemlocks lower down, the largest Alaska yellow-cedar in the world doesn't look very impressive. However, many hundreds of years are required for that species to attain such size.

The cedar is a good turnaround point. Above here the way steepens into a series of short switchbacks up to 1550-meter (5100-foot) Ipsut Pass. The most notable spot is a free shower bath from a waterfall under a tall cliff overhanging the trail.

This route is an alternate way to Tolmie Peak or Mowich Lake (Hike 11). From Ipsut Pass the lake is 2½km (1½ miles) to the left and the peak 3km (2 miles) to the right.

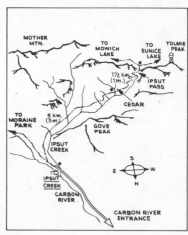

Largest known Alaska yellow-cedar tree

Marmot near Ipsut Pass

MOWICH LAKE AND CARBON RIVER

16 Seattle Park

Round trip 25km (16 miles)
Hiking time 9 hours
High point 1950 meters (6400 feet)
Elevation gain 1100 meters (3600 feet)
Snowfree mid-July
to mid-October

A picture-like parkland of heather meadows interspersed with groves of alpine trees. There are no campsites in Seattle Park, making this a long and very strenuous day hike. However, camping is permitted at a site in Cataract Valley at 1½km (1 mile) below the park.

Drive to the Carbon River Entrance and continue to road-end at Ipsut Creek Campground. Find the trail at the upper boundary of the camp.

Hike an easy 5km (3 miles) up the west side of the Carbon River, passing on the way a junction with a trail left across the river. Continue straight ahead, passing Carbon River Camp, to Cataract Creek and a junction; go right.

Now come 5km (3 miles) of steady climbing (in about 1½km, 1 mile, take time for a short side-trip to Cataract Falls), passing the Cataract Valley camp to the first open meadow. The trail in the forest is nicely graded until the last ¾km (½ mile), then becomes steep and muddy. Seattle Park starts at the foot of the first meadow, near the crossing of Marmot Creek. However, it's still another kilometer to wide-open country.

The trail continues another 3km (2 miles) to Spray Park, along the way crossing a permanent snowfield and topping a 1950-meter (6400-foot) ridge. From the park the trail goes on to Mowich Lake (Hike 12).

For an interesting side-trip, either from the ridge top or partway up, leave the trail and hike heather and rocky slopes to an overlook of the Carbon Glacier. Below is debris-covered ice of the lower glacier. Above is Willis Wall. Several delightful ponds are tucked in pockets. This viewpoint also can be reached from the saddle between Seattle and Spray Parks.

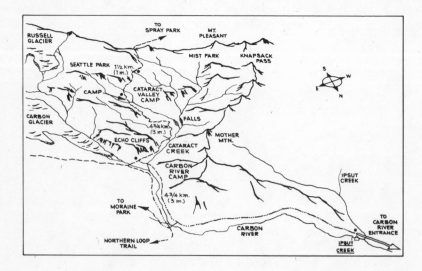

Mount Rainier from Seattle Park

MOWICH LAKE AND CARBON RIVER

17 Northern Loop And Natural Bridge

Loop trip 50½km (31½ miles)
Hiking time 4 days
High point 2055 meters (6740 feet)
Elevation gain 2590 meters (8500 feet)
Snowfree mid-July
to mid-October

A long loop hike through forests and meadows, over rivers, under a cliff of colorful rocks, near the dramatic Natural Bridge, past numerous mountain lakes, and with ever-changing views of the mountain and its glaciers. The first portion to Lake James can be done as an overnight trip.

Drive to the Carbon River Entrance and continue to road-end at Ipsut Creek Campground. Find the trail at the upper boundary of the camp.

The first 3km (2 miles) lie along the valley floor, close to river elevation. At a junction take the left fork across the Carbon River. The river often floods and frequently changes course, washing out the bridge; the exact point of the crossing therefore varies. On the far side of the river the Wonderland Trail turns right, the Northern Loop Trail left.

The way goes downvalley a short way, then begins an unrelenting 900-meter, 6½km (3000-foot, 4-mile) climb to Windy Gap. The first 5km (3 miles) are through forest on a smooth and soft path. No water! The last 1½km (mile) tends to be muddy, but the great open meadows compensate for any trouble. Above are Tyee Peak and the colorful Yellowstone Cliffs. Approaching Windy Gap one sees a pair of small lakes to the left and another to the right.

The open country of 1770-meter (5800-foot) Windy Gap (9½km, or 6 miles, from Ipsut Creek) offers wide views, well worth a long lunch stop.

A few hundred yards beyond Windy Gap is the side-trail to Natural Bridge, a 2¾km (1¾-mile) round trip. The bridge, about 30 meters (100 feet) high and 30 meters (100

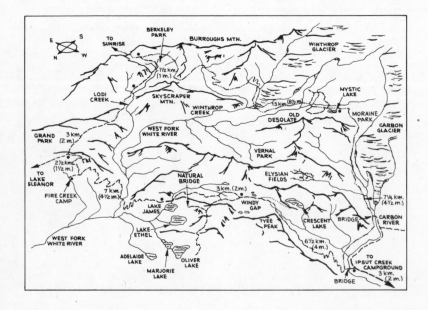

54

Natural Bridge

feet) long, is located in a difficult spot for good viewing, but is spectacular all the same. Better hurry; the bridge doesn't look strong enough to possibly remain standing another season.

Back on the Northern Loop Trail, descend in 3km (2 miles) to camps at Lake James, elevation 1330 meters (4370 feet). At 12½km (8 miles) from Ipsut Creek, this is the turnaround for overnighters. (If Lake James rather than the complete loop is the aim, start at Sunrise. The distance is greater but the elevation gain less.)

On the second day of the loop hike, drop to a crossing of the West Fork White River. Then begin a long climb of 760 meters (2500 feet), at 7km (4½ miles) passing Fire Creek Camp and the only water, at 9½km (6 miles) reaching a junction with the Grand Park trail (Hike 27). Continue 3km (2 miles) to a camp in lower Berkeley Park. Total distance from Lake James, 12½km (8 miles).

The third day climb 1½km (1 mile) from Berkeley Camp through meadows to a junction with the Wonderland Trail. Turn right and climb a bit more to a 2055-meter (6740-foot) pass below Skyscraper Mountain. Descend 650 meters (2140 feet) to the snout of the Winthrop Glacier and a crossing of Winthrop Creek, a tributary of the White River. Climb 370 meters (1200 feet) to Mystic Camp (Hike 18), at 15km (9½ miles) from lower Berkeley Park.

On the fourth day complete the loop by returning 9½km (6 miles) to Ipsut Creek via Moraine Park.

MOWICH LAKE AND CARBON RIVER

18 Moraine Park

Round trip to Mystic Lake 19km (12 miles)
Hiking time 6 hours
High point 1830 meters (6004 feet)
Elevation gain 1070 meters (3500 feet)
Snowfree mid-July
   to mid-October

A close look at the snout of the Carbon Glacier, lowest-elevation glacier in the old 48 states, flower meadows and high ridges for roaming, and a near view of enormous Willis Wall. If lucky, one may see avalanches seemingly float down the 1100-meter (3600-foot) cliff.

Drive to the Carbon River Entrance and continue to road-end at Ipsut Creek Campground. Find the trail at the upper boundary of the camp.

The first 5km (3 miles) lie on the valley floor close to river elevation. Pass the Northern Loop junction at 3km (2 miles), the Seattle Park junction at 5km (3 miles), and shortly beyond cross the Carbon River on a suspension bridge to another junction. Go right.

The trail now steepens, gaining 520 meters (1700 feet) in 3km (2 miles). The first portion on rubbly and cliffy slopes above the Carbon Glacier is very rough. Here are close views of the glacier snout; though some other glaciers in the Park have receded almost a mile in the last 30 years, the Carbon has held its own. A tumbling creek makes a good rest stop. Then the trail enters forest and becomes smooth, though still steep. The final stretch emerges in parkland and flattens out.

Officially, Moraine Park is the rather small meadow between trail and glacier, but hikers generally refer to Mystic Lake, Mineral Mountain, and the lower tree-and-flower slopes of Curtis Ridge as Moraine Park. The official Moraine Park is pretty enough in itself, especially in flower season, but the best is yet to come. Follow the trail upward a steep 1½km (1 mile) to an 1830-meter (6004-foot) saddle. From here one can drop to Mystic Lake and camps a short way beyond or hike up along Curtis Ridge for dramatic close-ups of Willis Wall and views over the Winthrop Glacier to Steamboat Prow.

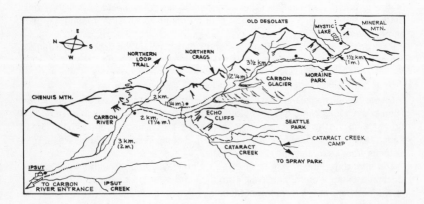

Willis Wall and Carbon Glacier

Owyhigh Lake and Governors Ridge

WHITE RIVER

19 Owyhigh Lakes

Round trip to lakes from White River 11km (7 miles)
Hiking time 3½ hours
High point 1555 meters (5100 feet)
Elevation gain 410 meters (1350 feet)
Snowfree mid-July through October

One way from White River to Deer Creek 13½ km (8½ miles)
Hiking time 5 hours
High point 1646 meters (5400 feet)
Elevation gain 660 meters (2170 feet)
Snowfree mid-July to mid-October

Alpine lakes surrounded by acres of wildflowers in the shadow of the ragged peaks of Governors Ridge.

There are two ways to reach the lakes: a 5½km (3½-mile) trail from the White River and an 8km (5-mile) trail from the road to Ohanapecosh. If transportation can be arranged, the two can be combined into a one-way hike; the best starting place for such a trip is the White River approach, since going this direction involves slightly less elevation gain.

Drive from the White River Entrance 3km (2 miles) to a parking area on the right, 1½km (1 mile) beyond Shaw Creek. The trail starts on the left side of the road and climbs steadily through the woods, the path wide and smooth with long switchbacks. At 5km (3 miles), ¾km (½ mile) short of the lakes, is Owyhigh Camp. The timber thins shortly before reaching the 1555-meter (5100-foot) lakes. To the east is craggy Governors Ridge. Directly west is Tamanos Peak.

From the lakes the trail climbs another 100 meters (300 feet) to a 1650-meter (5400-foot) pass with a view of Cowlitz Chimneys, then drops steadily but not steeply into Kotsuck Creek and down to the junction with the East Side Trail. In about 3km (2 miles) pass a viewpoint of a waterfall. In 5km (3 miles) cross Boundary Creek. Take time out to walk up the creek bed to a waterfall.

Save energy for the last ¾km (½ mile). At the junction with the East Side Trail, cross Chinook Creek, then Deer Creek, and take the Deer Creek trail, which climbs 120 meters (400 feet) to reach the highway.

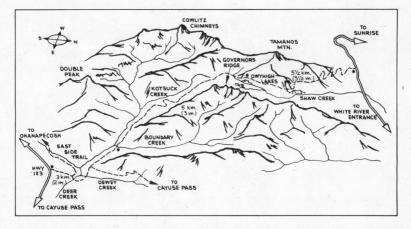

59

Round trip 13½km (8½ miles)
Hiking time 4 hours
High point 1800 meters (5920 feet)
Elevation gain 460 meters (1500 feet)
Snowfree July
   to October

One of the favorite hikes in the Park, on a wide path to an alpine meadow under the pinnacle of Little Tahoma. For those who don't wish to do the whole trip, the lower portion of the trail makes a fine forest walk. Many deep-woods flowers that by early summer have come and gone on the south side of the Park are just starting to bloom in this valley as late as the middle of August; especially notable is the queen's cup beadlily. This is one of the most crowded areas of the Park, with 300-400 hikers a day. Until the meadows recover from past overuse only a few campsites will be available. Wood fires are not permitted.

Drive from the White River Entrance 5km (3 miles) to a parking area just beyond the Fryingpan Creek bridge. The trail starts across the highway.

For 3km (2 miles) the way ascends gently in forest to a bluff overlooking Fryingpan Creek. Near the end of 4¾km (3 miles), pass through debris of a large avalanche and cross the creek. The final 1½km (1 mile) is steep, ending in a series of short switchbacks; here, during July-August, look for attractive displays of avalanche fawnlily.

The stone shelter cabin is in the grove to the left; northeast of it on a bench are good campsites. Little Tahoma dominates the meadows, rising above the Fryingpan Glacier to the southwest. West are the Emmons Glacier and Mount Rainier. North is Goat Island Mountain. East are the Sarvent Glaciers. South is Panhandle Gap.

If transportation can be arranged, a classic 2-3-day trip is over Panhandle Gap to Indian Bar (Hike 40) and on down to the Box Canyon on the Stevens Canyon Road, a total one-way distance of 25km (17 miles).

From Summerland climb 225 meters (840 feet) in less than 3km (2 miles) to 2060-meter (6750-foot) Panhandle Gap. A good share of this distance is through

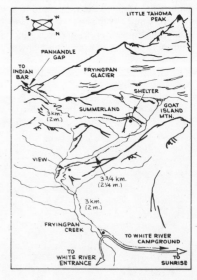

Sitka columbine

Mountain goats near Panhandle Gap

rough moraine, and a swift creek must be forded. From the Gap the trail traverses wintry and barren slopes above Ohanapecosh Park 2½km (1½ miles) before descending 3km (2 miles) to Indian Bar. This is the highest and most desolate section of the Wonderland Trail. Much of the way lies over large snowfields; though the route is marked by a few rock cairns, it is very easy to lose in a fog, not to mention a storm.

Inexperienced hikers should not attempt to travel this area early in the season or in bad weather. After spells of good weather, though, generally the track is clearly booted into the snow and can be followed quite safely if the only problem is a dense fog.

From Indian Bar proceed on out the Cowlitz Divide to Box Canyon.

Panhandle Gap demands a special note. Atop the Gap, look up and left to the Cowlitz Chimneys, volcanic plugs from old eruptions; except on very hot days, one may almost count on seeing mountain goats.

Mining relics in Glacier Basin

WHITE RIVER

21 Glacier Basin

Round trip 11km (7 miles)
Hiking time 4 hours
High point 1770 meters (5800 feet)
Elevation gain 390 meters (1280 feet)
Snowfree July
to October

A trip that offers no overwhelming view of the mountain, but more than compensates with the peaceful seclusion of a meadowy basin. The easy walk also displays artifacts of the Storbo Mine. From here, in 1894-5, "high-grading" prospectors took out ore samples valued by them at $450 a ton. In 1902 a copper claim was established, but despite sporadic speculative activity until 1957, nothing of commercial value was ever found. However, some of the basin is still privately owned—and a continuing threat to the natural integrity of the Park.

Drive from the White River Entrance 8km (5 miles) to the White River bridge and turn left on the gravel road to the White River Campground. Find the trail at the upper end of the camp.

The walking begins—and continues much of the way—on remnants of the miners' old wagon road, which was passable to automobiles as late as the 1940s. The open road is hot on sunny days, but runs close to the Inter Fork of the White River, with cool pools for drinking and splashing.

At 1½km (1 mile) is a junction with the Emmons Moraine trail, a ¾km (½-mile) side-trip to a view of the snout of the largest glacier in the conterminous 48 states. One must use imagination to be impressed by the heaps of rubble covering the glacial ice. There is, however, a good view of Little Tahoma rising above.

In 4km (2½ miles) pass the remains of the miners' sawmill and power plant. Here the trail leaves what's left of the mine road and climbs steeply into open meadows, then levels off and enters Glacier Basin.

Bands of goats prowl the high slopes. In season the basin floor is bright with flowers. A tiny bit of the mountain appears above The Wedge, topped by Mt. Ruth and Steamboat Prow. Splendid campsites.

Across the river are rotted timbers of the mine entrance, rusting equipment, and the site of another cabin. Higher in the valley are more holes, more junk. Much of the wooden litter in the flat, marshy meadow at the center of the basin disappeared in flames one night in the 1960s, gathered laboriously by anti-miner volunteers.

A climbers' track continues from the basin toward Interglacier, rising out of flowers and greenery into bouldery wastes of ice country.

If transportation can be arranged, Glacier Basin can be reached by an easy downhill trail from Sunrise (Hike 28), one-way hikers then going on out to the White River Campground.

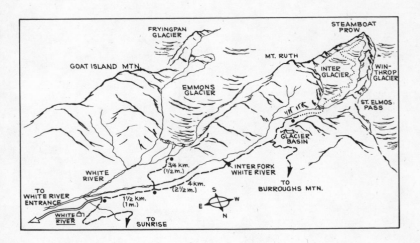

Palisades Lake

WHITE RIVER

22 Palisades Lakes

Round trip 11km (7 miles)
Hiking time 3 hours
High point 1890 meters (6200 feet)
Elevation gain (including return) 365
   meters (1200 feet)
Snowfree mid-July
   to mid-October

A series of at least seven lakes along the trail, all on the "dry" side of the mountain. Fishermen have known these lakes for years, but any hiker will enjoy them for their beautiful alpine settings. No views of the mountain, but an interesting rock formation called The Palisades. The trail has one bad feature: it drops 150 meters (500 feet) and then goes up and down, up and down.

Drive from the White River Entrance 16¾km (10½ miles) to the parking area at Sunrise Point. Cross the highway on the north side and look over the stone railing directly down at Sunrise Lake, the first of the series. The trail starts at the north end of the horseshoe bend.

The way follows the ridge down a short distance, then switchbacks toward Sunrise Lake. In ¾km (½ mile) the trail divides. The left fork leads to Sunrise Lake, the choice of most hikers and a good destination for a short walk. However, more and better lakes lie beyond, so take the right fork.

In 2½km (1½ miles) from the road the path skirts Clover Lake, largest of the chain. In 4km (2½ miles) are two unnamed lakes surrounded by woods. The trail continues another 1½km (1 mile), passing under the cliffs of The Palisades, ending at Palisades Lake.

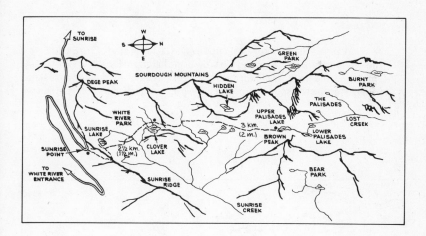

Round trip from ¾ to 6½km (½ to 4 miles)
Snowfree mid-July
through September

23 Sunrise Nature Trails

A glacier overlook, a walk high above the White River through a silver forest with views directly down on White River Campground, and a gem of a lake. Drive from the White River Entrance to Sunrise and take as many of these hikes as time and energy permit.

Sourdough Ridge Nature Trail

A self-guiding nature trail, starting on the north side of the picnic area and going in a loop, an easy hour's stroll, through meadows and along the ridge to fine views of Rainier and down to Huckleberry Park.

Emmons Vista Nature Trail

Find the ¾km (½-mile) trail directly across the parking lot from Sunrise Lodge, near the gravel road to the campground. At the start is a box containing copies of an interpretive pamphlet keyed to numbered posts along the way. At the end of the trail is an exhibit explaining the workings of a glacier.

Silver Forest

From Sunrise walk the Emmons Vista trail a short bit to the start of the Silver Forest trail. The way is fairly level, traversing the brow of the hill above the White River valley. Views of the mountain are unlimited; the silver forest, trees killed by fire and bleached by weather, offers picturesque foregrounds. Owls make their homes in the old snags.

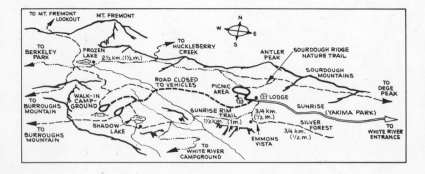

Little Tahoma and Emmons Glacier from Shadow Lake

Sunrise Rim Trail

At a junction in the Emmons Vista trail, turn right and contour along steep hillside with views of the mountain and White River. Pass junction with the Wonderland Trail which drops 4¾km (3 miles) to the White River. Shadow Lake is surrounded by groves of alpine trees and flowers in season. Views of Little Tahoma, though Mount Rainier is hidden. The lake is only a few meters (feet) from the hike-in campground. Return by the trail or the closed road.

A considerably more energetic (but worth it) alternate return is via the high trail visible up on the Sourdough Mountains. Follow the road and signs for the Wonderland Trail (west) from the campground back toward Sunrise. The way follows a long-abandoned road to Frozen Lake, the fenced water supply for facilities at Sunrise. After climbing 150 meters (500 feet) in less than ¾km (½ mile), reach the Wonderland Trail and pass to the right of the lake. Walk a long 1½km (1 mile) over a hump and along a sidehill, then drop through meadows to Sunrise.

Mount Rainier from Sourdough Mountain trail

WHITE RIVER

24 Sourdough Trail

Round trip 6½km (4 miles)
Hiking time 2 hours
High point 2135 meters (7006 feet)
Elevation gain 190 meters (600 feet)
Snowfree July
　　through September

An alpine ridge with a classic view of Mount Rainier. Look down on Sunrise Lodge and the busy highway. End at Sunrise Point parking lot. Along the way take a spur trail to the top of Dege Peak for a broad panorama of Cascade Crest summits to the east.

Drive from the White River Entrance to Sunrise. Sourdough Mountains are the long ridge of low peaks rising to the north. The trail leaves from the picnic area at a large sign. In a short distance pass a junction. Keep right, following signs for Dege Peak.

Soon the trail is joined by a rehabilitated, steep shortcut from the lodge. This latter was not built, but was the result of countless impatient hikers shortcutting the well-graded path. Thousands of hours of work by rangers and the Youth Conservation Corps have gone into replanting and restoring the shortcut to meadow.

The views get better and the crowds thinner the farther one goes out the ridge. The path stays near the crest, contouring around the higher summits. Where the track starts up Dege Peak, keep left at a junction for the final short bit to the top.

Horizons are unlimited. Mount Rainier is supreme, of course, but still must compete with the Sarvent Glaciers and Cowlitz Chimneys to the south. Far below is the White River and State 410, the highway over Chinook Pass. Farther north rise distant peaks of the Cascades and northwest are the Olympic Mountains. At the east base of the peak lie Sunrise and Clover Lakes (Hike 22), and on the northwest slopes are the green meadows of Huckleberry Park.

If transportation can be arranged, go back the short bit to the junction and take the trail 1½km (1 mile) down the ridge to Sunrise Point. However, if such an opportunity is available, it's more interesting to walk from Sunrise Point to Sunrise; this way the view is always in front. The trail starts on the uphill side of the highway from the parking area and follows the ridge. The Sunrise Point beginning adds 100 meters (300 feet) of elevation to the climb but the one-way hiking distance is only 5km (3 miles) instead of the 6½km (4-mile) round trip from Sunrise Lodge.

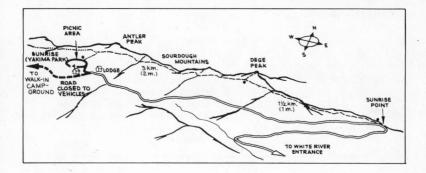

Huckleberry Creek

WHITE RIVER

25 Huckleberry Creek

One way 16km (10 miles)
Hiking time (downhill) 4 hours
High point 2042 meters (6700 feet)
Elevation loss 1070 meters (3500 feet)
Snowfree mid-July
   through September

Miles of forest walking within sound of the clear bubbling water of Huckleberry Creek, passing by numerous waterfalls, Forest Lake amid the trees, and finally a meadow basin and alpine ridge—a superb approach from low country to high country and one of the wildest and most respectful ways to experience the Park from bottom to top.

However, the trail (which probably predates the Park) was built by men in a hurry to get places and is very steep. Therefore, many hikers prefer to have their dessert first and then the main course and the soup and salad—which is to say, they start at the top in Yakima Park and descend to the bottom at the Huckleberry Creek road in Mt. Baker-Snoqualmie National Forest.

To do the one-way downhill trip, transportation must be arranged. Such as, drive in two cars from Enumclaw on State 410 to a junction with Forest Service road No. 186 and continue right 8¾km (5½ miles) almost to road-end. Leave one car at a small parking lot near Forest Service trail No. 1182, signed "Huckleberry Creek Trail—Park Boundary 1½ Miles." In the second car, drive to the White River Entrance and on to Sunrise.

Begin walking from the picnic area, as for Sourdough Mountains (Hike 24). In a short bit climb left on the Wonderland Trail ¾km (½ mile) to the ridge crest and a junction. Go right, dropping rapidly in a series of short switchbacks to a divide between an attractive meadow basin on the right and a cold and rocky cirque on the left. The trail switchbacks down into the cirque, crosses a tumbling headwater of Huckleberry Creek, swings around a shoulder to a second headwater, then falls into forest and 1723-meter (5653-foot) Forest Lake, with campsite.

The grade moderates a bit below the lake, but the next 5km (3 miles) still are pretty stiff. The lower reaches of the trail follow creek meanders along the valley bottom. At the Park boundary is an old patrol cabin fenced by huge windfalls which have missed it by inches; one year this relic of the past will be the target of a toppling tree.

The bottom-to-top-and-back-again round-trip 32km (20 miles) can be done without special transportation arrangements on a weekend backpack. Those who earn the high meadows by hiking the valley approach get some notion of how glorious it was to enter Yakima Park when it was wild; they pity travelers who arrive in automobiles.

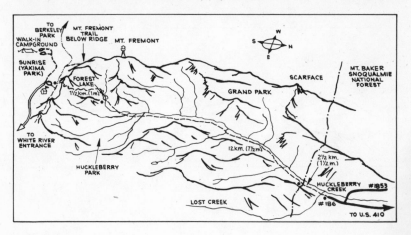

26 Mt. Fremont Lookout

Round trip 9km (5½ miles)
Hiking time 3 hours
High point 2195 meters (7200 feet)
Elevation gain 365 meters (1200 feet)
Snowfree mid-July
    through September

A fire lookout with the white glaciers of Mount Rainier on one side and the greenery of National Park and National Forest trees on the other.

Drive from the White River Entrance to Sunrise. From the picnic area follow the Wonderland Trail (west) 2½km (1.5 miles) to a junction of five trails, all well-marked. The lookout trail follows the west side of Frozen Lake and climbs around the hill to the north. The highest point of the trail is at the ridge corner. From here the way descends a hundred meters as it traverses ¾km (½ mile) to the lookout, which is not on the summit of Mt. Fremont.

South is The Mountain, north the long line of Cascades. On a clear day the Olympics appear, and with binoculars one can see the Space Needle in Seattle.

Closer are the flat expanse of Grand Park (Hike 27) and, beyond, the forests. Logging roads are being built by the Forest Service almost to the Park boundary; eventually the only virgin forest remaining will be that within the Park.

The lookout is occupied only during periods of extreme fire danger. If a ranger is on duty, he (or she) will be glad to explain duties and show how the fire-locator works. Ask him or her to point out the Natural Bridge on the Northern Loop (Hike 17); it appears quite small from here, but is visible when the sun is right. Please carry your own drinking water; there is none on the trail and the lookout should not be asked to give up any.

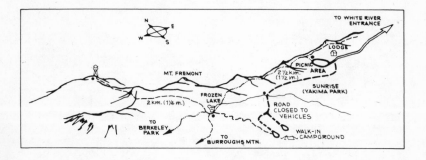

Mt. Fremont Lookout

WHITE RIVER

27 Grand Park

Round trip to Grand Park 21km (13 miles)
Hiking time 6 hours
High point 2042 meters (6700 feet)
Elevation gain (including return climb) 610
    meters (2000 feet)
Snowfree mid-July
    through September

In the up-and-down landscape of Mount Rainier, the almost flat, 3km-long (2-mile-long) plateau of Grand Park is a striking oddity. The explanation: many thousands of years ago a lava flow filled an ancient canyon; the displaced streams sought new courses at the edges of the flow, leaving the lava surface as a high tableland, which was later covered by a thick layer of pumice. A small herd of elk makes its home here and chances are good of seeing a genuinely "wild" (unaccustomed to humans) bear. An immense collection of flowers.

Drive from the White River Entrance to Sunrise. From the picnic area follow the Wonderland Trail (west) 2½km (1.5 miles) to a five-way junction. Continue on the Wonderland Trail west, across and down a pretty and varied series of meadows. In a little over ¾km (½ mile) is another junction. Keep right, dropping rapidly into Berkeley Park. Pass a series of springs (oozing ground, green lush plants). In lower Berkeley Park are loud and lovely waterfalls of Lodi Creek, a talus where marmots whistle from boulders, and a camp in the trees. The lookout on Mt. Fremont can be seen above.

The way descends in forest to 1585 meters (5200 feet), a total elevation loss from Frozen Lake of 460 meters (1500 feet) which must be regained on the return. Then it swings out of the valley onto a dividing ridge between trees of Lodi Creek and meadows of Cold Basin and climbs 100 meters (300 feet) to the edge of Grand Park, elevation about 1675 meters (5500 feet), at 10½km (6½ miles) from Sunrise.

The park provides unique foregrounds for views of The Mountain. No water except in early summer.

If the party plans to continue on the trail, the route stays along the west side of the meadow 1km (¾ mile) to the junction with the Northern Loop Trail (Hike 17), which goes left, in 2km (1¾ miles) dropping about 300 meters (1000 feet) to Fire Creek Camp. Keep right to Lake Eleanor, 5½km more (3½ miles), through grassy flats broken more and more by groves of trees (including many black snags killed by a 1965 forest fire). Shortly before the trail drops off the plateau, forest closes in. At first the descent is steep, then moderates.

Lake Eleanor, on the edge of the Park at 1520 meters (4985 feet), is surrounded by trees. Good camping. The stillness, however, may be broken by the roar of logging trucks on a Forest Service road less than 1km (¾ mile) away.

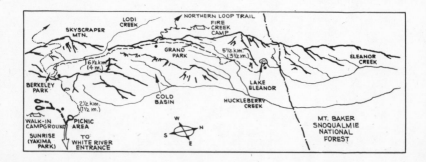

Grand Park and Mount Rainier

28 Burroughs Mountain

Round trip to Second Burroughs 8km (5 miles)
Hiking time 3 hours
High point 2255 meters (7400 feet)
Elevation gain 275 meters (900 feet)
Snowfree mid-July
   through September

If there is a trail between earth and heaven, this is it. The ridge of Burroughs Mountain, high above the White River, gives the impression of going easily onward and upward to the very tip of Columbia Crest.

Any part of the walk is superb, and the first section usually is crowded with travelers aged from less than 1 year to more than 70. As one goes along, the crowds dwindle.

Winthrop Glacier from Third Burroughs Mountain

Drive from the White River Entrance to Sunrise. The trail starts on the south side of the parking lot and goes to the Sunrise Campground.

From the campground the trail makes a stiff little climb to an overlook of the White River and Emmons Glacier—a good turnaround point for short-trippers—then continues up around a slope of slabby chunks of andesite (and a snowfield that lingers late and can be dangerous) and onto a wide, flat plateau. Burroughs Mountain, like Grand Park (Hike 27), is the remnant of a lava flow which filled an ancient canyon; the displaced streams carved valleys at the sides of the flow, leaving a tableland as yet relatively undissected. In less than 2½km (1½ miles) is the 2225-meter (7300-foot) high point of First Burroughs Mountain and the junction with the Wonderland Trail.

Another ¾km (½ mile) leads to 2255-meter (7400-foot) Second Burroughs and a memorial to Edmond S. Meany, long-time President of The Mountaineers. No water on the high ridge, but, in spite of it, small flowers and clumps of heather are scattered amid the volcanic rubble. North is the odd, green plateau of Grand Park. West are views toward the Carbon Glacier and Moraine Park.

Burroughs Mountain offers possibly the finest example of easily-accessible alpine vegetation in the Cascades. This plant community grows very, very slowly. The thin volcanic soil contains little nourishment and moisture is not held long for plants to use. The growing season is short and strong winds dry plants and carry pumice which abrades the vegetation.

In addition to struggling with these difficult environmental factors, this alpine vegetation is sometimes subjected to man's impact. Hiking off the trail causes crushing and breaking of plants, destroys seeds for future plant crops, and can reduce the small amount of organic matter in the thin topsoil. Moving rocks to make cairns or windbreaks exposes roots to drying and eventual death. Studies have shown that recovery from such stresses takes hundreds of years, even after all off-trail hiking is halted.

To vary the return, take the Wonderland Trail back to Sunrise via Frozen Lake (Hike 26). The distance is about the same as the other approach, and the views down into the greenery of Berkeley Park have a dream-like quality. However, an extremely steep snow slope makes this route unsafe until mid-August or so; ask the ranger before setting out. Often a path is shoveled through the snow slope.

From Second Burroughs Mountain the trail descends 3½km (2¼ miles) to the Glacier Basin trail (Hike 21), reaching it at a point 1km (¾ mile) from the basin and 4km (2½ miles) from the road at White River Campground.

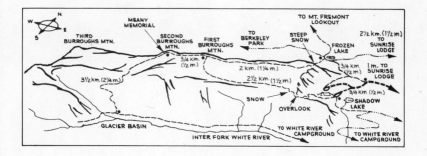

Upper Crystal Lake

CHINOOK PASS

29 Crystal Lakes

Round trip 9½km (6 miles)
Hiking time 3 hours
High point 1777 meters (5830 feet)
Elevation gain 700 meters (2300 feet)
Snowfree mid-June
   through October

Crystal-clear water surrounded by alpine flower fields. Elk are sometimes seen. And frequently dogs, which are more of a problem here than just about any place in the Park.

Drive east from Enumclaw on State 410 to the National Park boundary and continue 7¼km (4½ miles) to State Highway Department maintenance sheds. Park near here, but stay out of the workmen's way; they need most of the space for their machines. Find the trail close to where Crystal Creek goes into a culvert.

After a steady climb through forest, at a little more than 2½km (1½ miles) the trail crosses the base of an avalanche slope, up which it then makes a couple of long switchbacks. The third crossing gives the best look at the mountain, which disappears after that behind Crystal Peak (not to be confused with Crystal Mountain). In about 1½km (1 mile) from the avalanche pass lower Crystal Lake, and in ¾km (½ mile) more reach the 1777-meter (5830-foot) upper and larger lake.

A number of elk and mountain goat make their summer home in this area. Look for them on slopes around the upper lake. Note the rock formations to the east; through at least two windows in the rocks blue sky can be seen.

For better views of The Mountain, climb to the old lookout site on Crystal Peak. Find the trail at the end of a switchback about 2km (1¼ miles) from the highway.

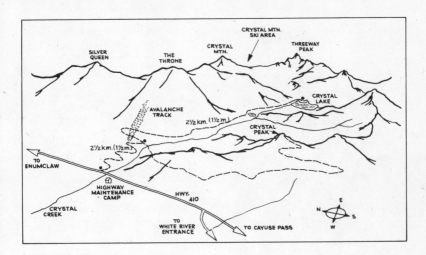

30 Deadwood Lakes

Round trip 5km (3 miles)
Hiking time 1½ hours
High point 1700 meters (5600 feet)
Elevation gain 215 meters (700 feet)
  including return
Snowfree July
  through October

Two mountain lakes surrounded by forest and meadows. The trail is not presently maintained and perhaps never will be again. Cross-country travel regulations currently apply, which means that for overnight trips a special permit is required and party size is limited to five.

Drive east from Enumclaw on State 410 to Chinook Pass. Park on the east side of the summit as close as possible to the trail overpass which marks the edge of the National Park. Parking is a problem—on a busy weekend a spot may have to be found as much as ¾km (½ mile) or more from the trailhead. If space here is full, there is a large parking area around a bend in the highway east. The way begins on the well-marked Pacific Crest Trail near the overpass.

Hike north on the Crest Trail as it slants downward, losing about 30 meters (100 feet) or more. In a little over ¾km (½ mile), as the trail is still dropping, note a well-defined but unmarked path angling slightly upward. This is the way to Deadwood Lakes. Evidently the trail was regularly maintained at one time, but that was long ago. Follow the path up to a 1700-meter (5600-foot) saddle and reenter the Park. The 1600-meter (5250-foot) lakes are visible below, down easy-walking meadows. Especially in foggy weather, a contour map is helpful in finding the route.

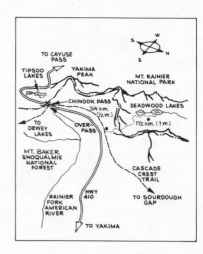

Gray jay

Deadwood Lakes and Mount Rainier

Mount Rainier from Naches Peak

CHINOOK PASS

31 Naches Peak Loop

Loop trip 8km (5 miles)
Hiking time 3 hours
High point 1770 meters (5800 feet)
Elevation gain 150 meters (500 feet)
Snowfree mid-July
    through October

An easy loop hike circling one of the guardians of Chinook Pass, passing through rich flower fields and beside two lakelets. Superb views of Rainier. Blueberries (usually) by late September. A magnificence of flaming color in autumn.

Drive east from Enumclaw on State 410 and park on the shoulder above Tipsoo Lake, just west of Chinook Pass.

The loop can be done in either direction, but going clockwise keeps Mount Rainier in front more of the time and thus is recommended. However, until late July or early August the trail along the east slopes of Naches Peak is quite snowy; unless a party is equipped for snow travel, it may then prefer to set out on the counterclockwise circuit, turning back when the country becomes too white and wet for personal tastes.

To start the clockwise loop, walk along the highway ¾km (½ mile) to the summit of Chinook Pass. Here intersect the Pacific Crest Trail and follow it over the highway on the wooden overpass. Small paths branch off left and right; stay on the main grade along the east side of Naches Peak, leaving the National Park and entering Mt. Baker-Snoqualmie National Forest.

The way traverses a steep sidehill above a green little valley, crossing several small waterfall-tumbling creeks—which, however, generally dry up in August. (There may then be no drinking water on the entire loop.) Flowers are at their prime roughly from late July to early August, but some bloom earlier, some later. About 1½km (1 mile) from Chinook Pass is an unnamed lakelet.

From the lakelet the trail ascends gently over a ridge which is the highest point of the loop, reenters the Park, and at 3km (2 miles) reaches a junction. The Pacific Crest Trail goes left, dropping to Dewey Lakes (excellent camping; see Hike 32).

The loop trail goes right, over a small rise to another unnamed lakelet reflecting Rainier. The way winds to high meadows on the west side of Naches Peak, Mount Rainier always in full view, and drops back to the highway near the parking lot.

The Naches Peak loop is among the most popular hikes in the Park. Even more popular, and a pleasure for anyone who can walk at all, no matter how slowly, are the beginning segments, which in a few hundred feet or any longer distance offer as nice a combination of flower-sniffing and mountain-gazing as one can find anywhere.

For a whole new experience of high meadows and The Mountain, do the loop on a moonlight night in late August or early September. Listen for the bugling of bull elk.

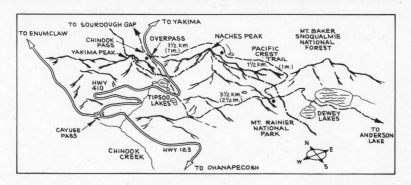

Dewey Lakes and shoulder of Seymour Peak

CHINOOK PASS

32 Pacific Crest Trail

One way from Chinook Pass to
Ohanapecosh Highway 29km (18 miles)
Hiking time 2-3 days
High point 1770 meters (5800 feet)
Elevation gain 460 meters (1500 feet)
Elevation loss 1555 meters (5100 feet)
Snowfree mid-July
through October

The Pacific Crest Trail extends from Canada to Mexico and in 1968 was acknowledged as an American classic when Congress gave it status as a National Scenic Trail.

The portion of the Crest Trail running along the east boundary of the Park (with frequent swings out into Mt. Baker-Snoqualmie National Forest) goes up and down, sometimes in subalpine forest but mostly in meadows, passing numerous lakes and ponds, waterfalls and flower fields. Occasional views of Mount Rainier, other views into peaks and valleys within the proposed Cougar Lakes Wilderness.

Whether a group is planning to hike this entire segment of the Crest Trail or only a part, the best starting point is 1645-meter (5040-foot) Chinook Pass—rather than the 580-meter (1900-foot) trailhead deep in the Ohanapecosh valley. (Good access is also available from the Crystal Mountain Ski Area, on National Forest land.) To do the one-way hike recommended, transportation must be arranged.

Drive east from Enumclaw on State 410 to Chinook Pass and park in the first available space just east of the summit. Cross the highway on the wooden overpass and hike south a scant 3km (2 miles) to the Dewey Lakes junction (Hike 31).

Descend 210 meters (700 feet) in a long ¾km (½ mile) to Dewey Lakes, at 1555 meters (5100 feet). Camping is now banned within 30 meters (100 feet) of the water by Forest Service regulations, which means most of the old camps around the meadow-and-forest-and-rockslide shores must **not** be used. The lakes make a fine destination for beginning hikers and small children; the round-trip distance from Chinook Pass is only 8km (5 miles), an easy weekend.

From Dewey Lakes the trail climbs past a wide meadow-marsh laced with meander-

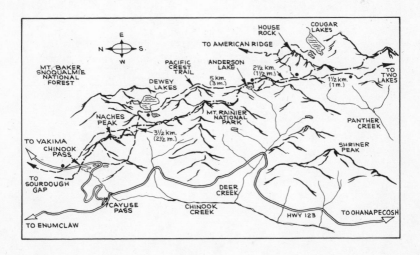

Pacific
Crest Trail
(Cont'd.)

ing streams, then rounds a shoulder of Seymour Peak. At 8¾km (5½ miles) is little Anderson Lake, with meadowy shores and forests on all sides. This is a good turnaround point for a long day's round-trip hike from Chinook Pass.

The trail climbs steeply a few hundred feet from Anderson Lake around the headwaters of Deer Creek, with views of Mount Rainier, then drops a bit to a junction (11km, 7 miles) with the American Ridge-Cougar Lakes trail. Next is a set of switchbacks up the forested west side of House Rock, above the headwaters of Panther Creek, into flowers again. At 15km (9½ miles) the way crosses the crest and contours above Two Lakes. At about 16km (10 miles) a side-trail descends 100 meters (300 feet) to the lakes and a campsite. The main trail continues to a junction at 17½km (11 miles) with the Laughingwater Creek Trail (Hike 36), which descends 11km (7 miles) to the highway near Ohanapecosh.

From the junction, the Crest Trail leaves the Park for good and continues south 24km (15 miles) to White Pass.

Camping at Dewey Lakes, Two Lakes, and Three Lakes (backcountry use permit needed for this camp).

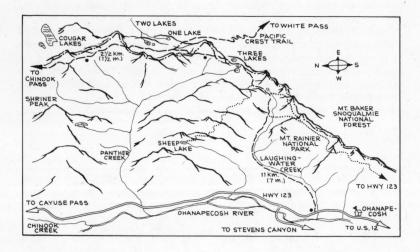

Deer near Two Lakes

OHANAPECOSH

33 East Side Trail

One way from Deer Creek to Ohanapecosh
14½km (9 miles)
Hiking time 4 hours
High point 1065 meters (3500 feet)
Elevation loss 460 meters (1500 feet)
Snowfree June
   to mid-November

A forest hike near a cool river. Try it in spring when higher trails are still buried under snow or in summer when The Mountain is lost in rain or in late fall when meadowlands are a blank misery of cold-blowing storm. A wide path with little brush to moisturize clothing.

If transportation can be arranged, this is an ideal one-way trip. Start at the top and walk downhill; except for the first ¾km (½ mile), the grade is so gentle a hiker hardly is aware of descending.

Drive north 9½km (6 miles) from the Stevens Canyon Entrance, or south 8km (5 miles) from Cayuse Pass, to a very small parking space ¾km (½ mile) south of Deer Creek. Sign on the west side of the road.

The trail drops rapidly a short ¾km (½ mile) to a nice campsite at the junction of Deer Creek and Chinook Creek. Here the way is joined by the East Side Trail, descending from Cayuse Pass and Chinook Pass. (For an even longer one-way hike, pick up this trail at either pass and follow it on down—to the total one-way distance add 8¾km, 5½ miles, from Chinook, 6½km, 4 miles, from Cayuse.)

In 1½km (1 mile) from Deer Creek cross Chinook Creek above a pretty canyon and falls. In about 5km (3 miles) cross the Ohanapecosh over a corkscrew of a falls. About 10½km (6½ miles) pass a side-trail to the Grove of the Patriarchs (Hike 35). In a little over 11km (7 miles) cross the Stevens Canyon Road and in another ¾km (½ mile) join the Silver Falls trail (Hike 37) and hike either side of the river into Ohanapecosh Campground.

Mostly the walk is out of sight of the river, but never out of sound. Sometimes the way is through virgin forest, occasionally crossing an avalanche slope covered with vine maple.

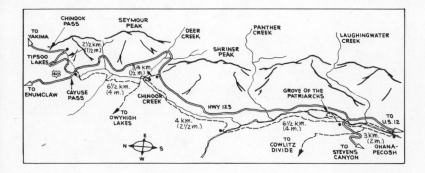

Trail bridge across Chinook Creek

OHANAPECOSH

34 Shriner Peak

Round trip to Shriner Peak 12¾km (8 miles)
Hiking time 5 hours
High point 1778 meters (5834 feet)
Elevation gain 1047 meters (3434 feet)
Snowfree July
through October

A lookout peak with a commanding view of the Ohanapecosh valley and Mount Rainier, and distant views of the Cascades north and south. A meadow lake in a basin below, summer home of a large herd of elk.

Drive north 5½km (3½ miles) from the Stevens Canyon Entrance, or south 12km (7½ miles) from Cayuse Pass, to the parking area on the west side of the road about ¾km (½ mile) north of the Panther Creek bridge. The trail and sign are on the east side of the road, both almost hidden from sight.

On sunny days it is best to start early in the morning to beat the heat. The dusty trail swings steeply from cool forest to hot hillside, climbing through an old burn almost devoid of trees and completely lacking in shade. In 4km (2½ miles) the way reaches the crest of a ridge; still no shade, but the view—and possible breeze—make the rest of the hike bearable. Along the ridge ¾km (½ mile) is the water supply for the lookout. From here the last 1½km (1 mile) switchbacks to the 1778-meter (5834-foot) summit.

The ranger at the lookout will be happy to provide a tour of his (or her) glass house and explain how the instruments work. Though the highway is directly below, this is one of the loneliest lookouts in the Park, with only a few dozen visitors some years.

Camping is permitted near the top of Shriner Peak. Water may have to be hauled some distance. Campers definitely will want to get up early to watch the sunrise reflected on Rainier's shining glaciers.

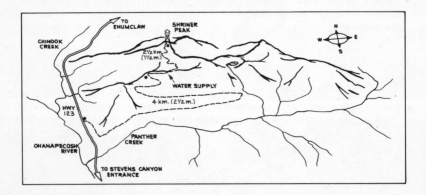

Air view of Shriner Peak and Mount Rainier

Grove of the Patriarchs

35 Grove Of The Patriarchs

Round trip 2½km (1½ miles)
Hiking time 1 hour
High point 670 meters (2200 feet)
Elevation gain none
Snowfree June
   through October

The name tells the story: a virgin forest of ancient Douglas-firs, western hemlocks, and western redcedars, a place to become humble in the presence of living things that were already aged—by human measure—when the Normans conquered England. Short and easy walk along a nature trail.

Drive to the Stevens Canyon Entrance and continue ⅓km (¼ mile) on the Stevens Canyon Road to a large parking lot beyond the Ohanapecosh River bridge. Trail starts behind the restrooms.

The way goes upstream through beautiful forest ¾km (½ mile) to a junction. The nature trail turns right, across a suspension bridge onto an island in the Ohanapecosh River. After passing through small trees, the path forks: go either way; it's a loop. Signs identify plants and describe features of the ecological community.

Isolated on the island and thus protected from fire, the trees have grown to gigantic proportions. In this small area are 20 western redcedars more than 7.5 meters (25 feet) in circumference; among them is the largest cedar in the Park. There are 10 Douglas-firs over 7.5 meters (25 feet) in circumference; one is 10.5 meters (35 feet). The trees are estimated to be nearly 1000 years old.

Giant cedar tree in Grove of the Patriarchs

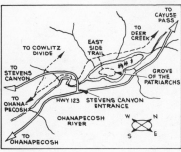

36 Three Lakes Trail (Laughingwater Creek)

Round trip to Three Lakes 19km (12 miles)
Hiking time 6 hours
High point 1525 meters (5000 feet)
Elevation gain 823 meters (2700 feet)
Snowfree July
    through October

A woods trail to three small lakes and onward to the Pacific Crest Trail. Or one can take either of two side-trips to some of the lonesomest country in the Park. Or hike an easy 1½km (mile) through the moss-covered forest to a resting place by the truly "laughing water" of the creek.

Drive about 1½km (1 mile) north from Ohanapecosh, or 1¼km (a short mile) south from the Stevens Canyon Entrance, to Laughingwater Creek. Park on the west shoulder of the highway north of the creek. Trail starts on the east side of the road just beyond a steep bank.

The first 1½km (1 mile), with a smooth tread and gentle grade, climbs steadily over a small knoll and then drops a few centimeters (inches). For those wanting a short hike this is the turnaround point. But before going back, walk down to the creek for a rest or a picnic—noisy but relaxing.

For the next 3km (2 miles) the way climbs easily; water is scarce in late summer. Gradually the trail becomes steeper, crossing a small creek at about 5½km (3½ miles).

At 7km (4½ miles) is a junction with a spur going right, to the East Boundary Trail. In about 8¾km (5½ miles) is the main junction with the East Boundary Trail, which is occasionally used by rangers on patrol duty. (The track is difficult to find in places and easily mistaken for one of the numerous game traces. No special views—just a chance to be alone. If contemplating hiking the trail, ask the Ohanapecosh ranger for the latest information.)

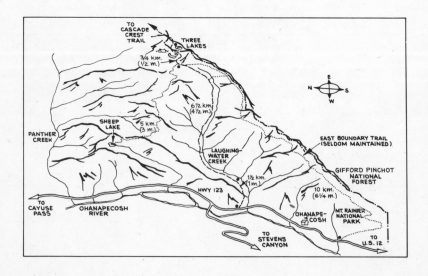

In 150 meters (500 feet) from the main East Boundary Trail junction pass a swamp and a junction, left, to Sheep Lake, 5km (3 miles) away on a seldom-used trail, rather sketchy in places, with occasional yellow paint marks, but generally following the ridge crest, climbing over numerous knolls. Sheep Lake, a shallow pool in a small meadow at an elevation of 1415 meters (4640 feet), is one of the more private places in the Park. A small elk herd summers in this area.

From the Sheep Lake junction the Laughingwater trail drops in ¾km (½ mile) to 1478-meter (4850-foot) Three Lakes. The patrol cabin, a log structure, is in a picturesque setting between the first and second lakes. Nearby is the camp area.

Follow the trail along the middle lake about 60 meters (a few hundred feet) to the Park boundary and the third lake. Continue ¾km (½ mile), climbing from trees into open country. For views of Mount Rainier hike another 1½km (1 mile) to the junction with the Pacific Crest Trail (Hike 32).

Patrol cabin at Three Lakes

Silver Falls on the Ohanapecosh River

37 Silver Falls

Loop trip 5km (3 miles)
Hiking time 1½ hours
High point 640 meters (2100 feet)
Elevation gain 100 meters (300 feet)
Snowfree May
    through November

Tall virgin forest, a moss-carpeted floor, and a busy waterfall in the Ohanapecosh River. All on an easy loop hike up the east bank of the river, returning down the west side of the valley.

Drive into the Ohanapecosh Campground and park in front of the Visitor Center. The trail starts behind the Center on the Ohanapecosh Hot Springs Nature Trail. In ¹/₃km (¼ mile) is a junction; go right on the Silver Falls trail, passing hot springs that years ago supported a health resort.

An easy grade follows within sound, if not sight, of the Ohanapecosh River, crossing Laughingwater Creek and climbing over a small bluff to a view of Silver Falls. (If the falls are one's only interest, they can be reached more quickly by taking the Laughingwater Trail from the highway, starting at a point 100 meters north of the Laughingwater Bridge.)

At the falls the loop trail bridges a narrow rock-walled canyon, crossing from the east side of the river to the west. Look down into a deep, crystal-clear pool. The way continues upstream to a scenic overlook at the top of the falls, then a few steps more to a junction with the East Side Trail (Hike 33). Keep left to another junction within a hundred steps. Keep left again. The trail, though now headed downstream, climbs a bit before descending to the starting point.

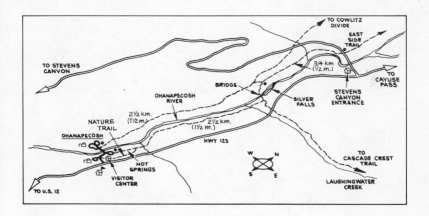

38 Cowlitz Divide

Round trip 12¾km (8 miles)
Hiking time 4 hours
High point 1450 meters (4760 feet)
Elevation gain 745 meters (2440 feet)
Snowfree July
    through September

Climb in deep-shadowed virgin forest to a junction with the Wonderland Trail. The route is often used, in combination with the Owyhigh Lakes trail (Hike 19) and East Side Trail (Hike 33), by hikers doing the Wonderland Trail but wishing to avoid the high, snowy country of Panhandle Gap (Hike 20).

Drive from the Stevens Canyon Entrance 1 kilometer (less than a mile) on the Stevens Canyon Road to a parking area and trail sign on the right.

(The hike can also begin at Ohanapecosh Campground, though this adds 3km, 2 miles, each way: from the campground follow the Silver Falls trail on the east side of the river, Hike 37; at the falls, cross the footbridge; in a few steps take a left fork and go 100 meters to another junction; take the right fork and in ¹/₃km, ¼ mile, reach the Stevens Canyon Road at the parking area.)

The first 1½km (1 mile) from the parking area is very moderate, gaining 120 meters (400 feet) through large trees. After a huge log bridge over a small creek, the way steepens, crossing Olallie Creek (campsites nearby) in about 5km (3 miles) and in another 1½km (1 mile) joining the Wonderland Trail a bit before it begins the long drop into Nickel Creek. No mountain views at this turnaround point, but the forest is reward enough.

If transportation can be arranged, a one-way trip can be made, continuing on out Backbone Ridge (Hike 39) or Nickel Creek (Hike 40).

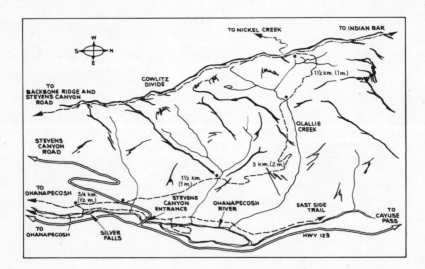

Bridge on Cowlitz Divide trail

39 Backbone Ridge

Round trip 13km (8 miles)
Hiking time 4 hours
High point 1555 meters (5100 feet)
Elevation gain 550 meters (1800 feet)
Snowfree July
through September

A chance for solitude on an infrequently-maintained trail used more by elk than people. Views are few but hikers are fewer. At times the path is very faint and often may be confused with game traces. The trip is all in small timber, with only glimpses through the trees of the Tatoosh Range and Mount Rainier.

Drive from the Stevens Canyon Entrance 10½km (6½ miles) on the Stevens Canyon Road to the large parking lot where the road swings around the end of Backbone Ridge. Find the trail on the uphill (north) side near the cut.

The first long kilometer is along the crest of the ridge. Then the way drops 100 meters to pass under cliffs on the west side of a high knoll. From here it gradually regains the ridge.

Stevens Peak from Backbone Ridge

In some 4km (2½ miles) are intersections with unmarked trails: the one coming up from the east is the old Cowlitz Divide trail from Packwood; the one from the west is more recent, built by blister-rust work crews. Note these junctions carefully; they could easily cause confusion on the descent.

In about 6½km (4 miles) pass St. Jacobs Lake and several campsites; $^1/_3$km (¼ mile) beyond is the junction with the Wonderland Trail, one leg of which proceeds straight ahead up the ridge toward Indian Bar while the other drops left into Nickel Creek.

If transportation can be arranged, a one-way trip can be made, going out the Cowlitz Divide trail (Hike 38) or Nickel Creek (Hike 40).

An alternate route up Backbone Ridge is the blister-rust trail, difficult to locate but an even better place to see elk and deer, the principal users of the path. Drive approximately 3km (2 miles) toward Paradise from the Backbone viewpoint. Just beyond a large road cut find the unmarked beginning. In $^1/_3$km (¼ mile) the trail passes the tent frames of a former blister-rust camp and in less than 1½km (1 mile) joins the Backbone Ridge trail below prominent cliffs. A very old and easily-missed sign at this junction is nailed on an 8-inch Pacific silver fir.

All these trails are easier to follow up than down.

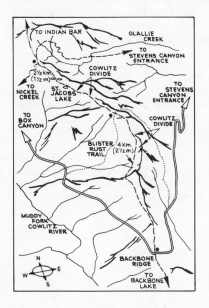

*Mount Rainier and Stevens Canyon
Road from Backbone Ridge*

STEVENS CANYON

40 Indian Bar

Round trip 23½km (14½ miles)
Allow 2 days
High point 1802 meters (5914 feet)
Elevation gain 670 meters (2200 feet) in,
    305 meters (1000 feet) out
Snowfree late July
    through September

A unique section of the Wonderland Trail. Miles of ridge-walking through alpine meadows with views of the southeast side of Mount Rainier, ending in a broad green valley into which pour a dozen waterfalls. One of the legendary places in the Park. A great spot to sit in the moonlight on a late-August night and listen to the bull elk bugling.

Drive the Stevens Canyon Road west from the Stevens Canyon Entrance 16km (10 miles), or east 17½km (11 miles) from the Longmire-Paradise road, to the parking lot at Box Canyon. Find the signed gravel trail directly across the highway from the parking area. (Do not take the paved nature trail by mistake.)

The first 1½km (1 mile) is easy walking on a moderate grade to Nickel Creek. Good campsites along the stream and on the far bank. In another ¾km (½ mile) is a small creek, the last reliable water before Indian Bar; fill canteens. From Nickel Creek the way climbs steadily to the Cowlitz Divide, reaching the crest in a bit less than 5km (3 miles) from the road. Here are junctions with the Backbone Ridge trail (Hike 39) and the trail from Ohanapecosh (Hike 38).

The next 7km (4½ miles) are along the crest of the Cowlitz Divide, going up and over some bumps and contouring around others. At times the way is very steep. First there are glimpses of the mountain through trees. Then the trail climbs higher, the meadows grow larger, and finally, atop a 1802-meter (5914-foot) knoll, the mountain comes completely and grandly into the open. To the southeast is Bald Knob. Beyond is Shriner Peak. From the knoll the trail drops 240 meters (800 feet) to 1560-meter (5120-foot) Indian Bar.

The Ohanapecosh River divides the large green meadow. The shelter cabin is on the west side of the river. At the valley head are small remnants of the Ohanapecosh Glacier. In early summer numerous waterfalls splash down the lava cliffs. Just 30 meters (100 feet) below the shelter is Wauhaukaupauken Falls, a name almost larger than the falls.

Don't forget the considerable elevation gain on the return hike.

If transportation can be arranged, Indian Bar can be combined with Summerland (Hike 20) for a one-way trip of 27km (17 miles), and a beauty.

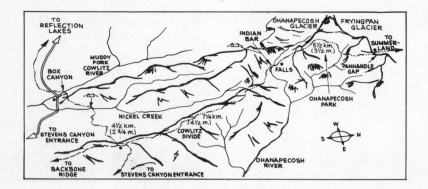

Trail shelter at Indian Bar

STEVENS CANYON

41 Bench And Snow Lakes

Round trip 3½km (2½ miles)
Hiking time 1 hour
High point 1426 meters (4678 feet)
Elevation gain 100 meters (300 feet)
Snowfree July
    through October

A trail with numerous ups and downs, very dusty in dry weather, traversing through a silver forest which in autumn offers the red of mountain-ash and huckleberries and some years a spectacular display of bear grass.

Drive the Stevens Canyon Road west from the Stevens Canyon Entrance 25½km (16 miles), or east 5km (3 miles) from the Longmire-Paradise road, to a parking area about 1½km (1 mile) east of Louise Lake. Find the trail here.

The two lakes lie at about the same elevation as the parking lot; however, several low ridges must be crossed on the way through meadows and a large "silver forest," caused by a fire that killed, but did not consume, the standing trees.

Bench Lake, at 1km (¾ mile), lies on the edge of a cliff amid dense thickets of slide alder.

In another ¾km (½ mile) is Snow Lake, occupying a cirque below Unicorn Peak. Around the shores are open meadows and groups of subalpine fir. To see Mount Rainier, walk to the far side. The lake frequently doesn't melt free of snow until late July. Unicorn Peak, highest point of the Tatoosh Range at 2115 meters (6939 feet), rises directly to the south.

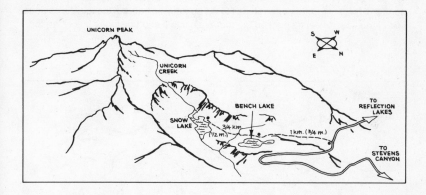

Snow Lake and Unicorn Peak

STEVENS CANYON

42 Pinnacle Saddle And Plummer Peak

Round trip to Plummer Peak 5km (3 miles)
Hiking time 2-3 hours
High point 1920 meters (6300 feet)
Elevation gain 460 meters (1500 feet)
Snowfree August
through September

A grand viewpoint of the mountain, far enough away to see it all in a single wide-eyed look, close enough to see fine detail of glaciers and lava cliffs.

Drive the Stevens Canyon Road west from the Stevens Canyon Entrance 28km (17½ miles), or east 2½km (1½ miles) from the Longmire-Paradise road, to the Reflection Lakes parking area. The trail starts on the uphill (south) side.

The path is gentle at first, but soon turns steep and remains so. In July several hazardous snowfields must be crossed. Use extreme caution; hikers lacking good boots would do better to give up and try again later in the season, when the snow has melted.

The view of Mount Rainier grows steadily more impressive with every foot of elevation gained; at the 1830-meter (6000-foot) saddle is an almost equally impressive view south to Mt. Adams.

The trail ends at the saddle. Yet countless tourists, many in street shoes, continue to the top of 2000-meter (6562-foot) Pinnacle Peak. Though trained climbers consider Pinnacle an easy ascent, most of the hikers who visit the summit have no business on the steep, unstable rock. They are a hazard to themselves with their slippery shoes—and a hazard to others below as they kick down loose stones.

The view from 1920-meter (6300-foot) Plummer Peak, west of the saddle, is just as good and far safer. Follow open slopes to the summit; no trail, but the route is obvious. Look for a little reflecting pool on the mountainside a short distance below the top.

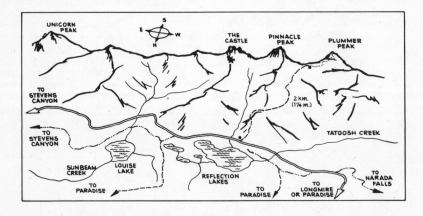

Mount Rainier from a small tarn on side of Plummer Peak

Seed pod of the western anemone

PARADISE AREA

43 Paradise Flower Trails

At Paradise the alpine flower fields reach a climax unsurpassed anywhere in the Cascades. All are easily reached on paved trails. One walk has a bonus: a view out over the Nisqually Glacier. Drive to the large parking lot near the Paradise Ranger Station and choose your trail for the day.

> Round trip 1½-5km (1-3 miles)
> Hiking time 1-3 hours
> High point 1800 meters (5900 feet)
> Elevation gain 150 meters (500 feet)
> Snowfree mid-July
> to mid-October

Flower Trails

Snow doesn't leave the meadows until mid-July, but even in June flowers bloom on exposed ridges, including a large field of yellow glacier lilies on the south side of Alta Vista. A few days after the snow melts away the meadows turn white again with avalanche lilies then blue with lupine and red with Indian paintbrush. In August the vast carpets of color give way to small patches of asters, gentians, and many other flowers.

Trails radiate from the Visitor Center, Paradise Inn, and the Ranger Station. All are good. Especially recommended is the walk to the top of Alta Vista, the green knoll directly above the Inn. The trail up the front side is extremely steep; stay to the left and approach the knoll from the far side. From the 1800-meter (5900-foot) top one can look down to Paradise, across to the Tatoosh Range, and out to Mt. Adams and Mt. St. Helens.

Moraine Trail

Round trip 3km (2 miles)
Hiking time 1½ hours
Elevation gain 120 meters (400 feet) going,
 60 meters (200 feet) on return
Snowfree July
 through September

Flowers along the edge of the Nisqually Glacier generally bloom a week or so later than those on Alta Vista. Relatively few people take this trail; a good chance for solitude.

Hike the paved trail around the west side of Alta Vista, cross a small creek, and continue a few hundred feet to a knoll and trail sign. Take the left-hand fork toward the glacier and find the trail leading down through a grove of trees. Drop 100 meters to the moraine. The way may be muddy but the best flowers are at the end. Return by the same route.

Nisqually Vista

Round trip 2km (1¼ miles)
Hiking time 1 hour
Elevation gain 60 meters (200 feet) on
 return
Snowfree July
 through September

Find the trail from the parking lot 100 meters south of the Visitor Center. The beginning is on stone steps. At an intersection in a few feet, keep left.

After ⅓km (¼ mile) the trail drops to a glacier viewpoint on the edge of the canyon. The glacier is descending from the summit like a slow-moving river. Snow accumulates at the higher elevations faster than it melts, growing hundreds of feet deep and compressing into ice pushing downhill at 10 or more inches a day. Some years the snout advances a few feet; other years it recedes. Compare the present position with the photograph on this page taken in 1968.

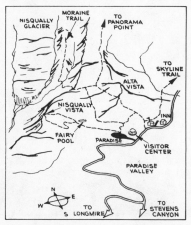

Snout of Nisqually Glacier as photographed in 1968

Tatoosh Range and Mount Adams from Panorama Point

PARADISE AREA

44 Skyline Trail

Loop trip 8km (5 miles)
Hiking time 3 hours
High point 2100 meters (6900 feet)
Elevation gain 520 meters (1700 feet)
Snowfree late July
  to mid-October

Walk through meadows above the Nisqually Glacier to a high overlook of Paradise Valley with views of far-off Mt. Adams and Mt. St. Helens. A good place to watch avalanches in the Nisqually Icefall and marmots lazing in the sun.

Drive to the large parking lot near the Paradise Ranger Station. The trail starts on the stone steps left of the restrooms or in front of Paradise Inn.

The first ¾km (½ mile), paved, climbs steeply around the west side of Alta Vista. Beyond blacktop the way continues up the ridge toward the mountain. Bypass the signed "Glacier Vista"; a little farther up the trail, a bit more than 1½km (1 mile) from the parking lot, is an even better look over the Nisqually Glacier. A long switchback leads to Panorama Point, aptly named.

Views of other volcanoes to the south open up beyond the Tatoosh Range. Mt. Adams, 72km (45 miles) to the southeast, has an appearance similar to Mount Rainier; the symmetrical cone of Mt. St. Helens, 74km (46 miles) to the southwest, looks remarkably like Japan's Fujiyama. On a clear day Mt. Hood, 154km (96 miles) away in Oregon, can be seen. To the east of Mt. Adams are Goat Rocks, the eroded roots of still another once-mighty volcano.

From Panorama Point the trail switchbacks a short way higher through volcanic rubble and glacial debris (many hikers instead cross a short permanent snowfield), then drops gradually in 1½km (1 mile) to the Golden Gate Trail (Hike 46), which can be used as a shorter alternate return to Paradise.

The Skyline Trail continues 1km (¾ mile) down the ridge to the Stevens-Van Trump Memorial, where another trail branches off left to the Paradise Ice Caves (Hike 46). The Skyline Trail continues only a short distance farther down the ridge before dropping into Paradise Valley. A 100-meter climb from the valley to Myrtle Falls, then a ¾km (½-mile) paved trail, complete the return to Paradise.

Until early August, at least, parts of the trail are covered by snow, requiring hiking boots—unlike the paved flower walks of Paradise.

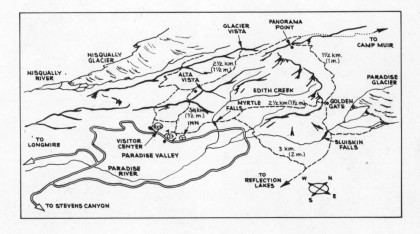

111

45 Camp Muir

Round trip 14½km (9 miles)
Hiking time 8 hours
High point 3048 meters (10,000 feet)
Elevation gain 1370 meters (4500 feet)
Recommended June
    through September

A long, arduous, and potentially hazardous ascent to the overnight cabin used by summit climbers. Climb through flowers, then rocks, then perpetual snow. At nearly 3km (2 miles) above sea level, look down on the Tatoosh Range, over the southern Cascade Mountains, and far into Oregon.

Take note: though hundreds of casual walkers go to Muir each year, this is not a trail hike. Much of the way is on snow. Part is over a permanent snowfield which is often crevassed in August and September. The mountain is notorious for "making its own weather"—mostly bad. On a clear day, without warning, clouds may form, enveloping hikers in blowing fog and wiping out all landmarks. At high elevation the temperature may fall abruptly, and the wind rise, and a balmy afternoon turn swiftly into a killing night. (See the discussion of hypothermia in the Introduction.)

Drive to the large parking lot near the Paradise Ranger Station. Before starting, sign the special Camp Muir register at the station; upon return, sign out. Follow the Skyline Ridge trail (Hike 44) 2½km (1½ miles). On the side of the long switchback on Panorama Point, find a trail that climbs steeply beside a small creek. The sign says, "Camp Muir 2.7 miles." (4.3 meters) But don't feel too encouraged; for the average hiker, Muir is still 4 hours away. (The 2.7 miles must be "air miles." They couldn't be "as the crow flies" since even a bird would have to circle a few times to gain all that elevation.)

The trail continues ¾km (½ mile) to Pebble Creek, a good spot to stop for a bite to eat and to fill water bottles. From here on there is no trail and the route is over steep, unbroken snowfields which can be hot and exhausting. An alternate route turns off the trail before Pebble Creek. This ridge route stays high, traversing around the side of

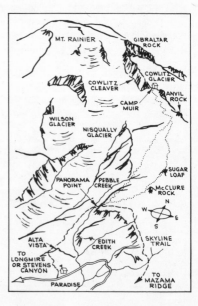

Climber above Camp Muir

Camp Muir, Cowlitz Glacier, and Gibraltar Rock

McClure Rock and over the rock ridge of Sugarloaf. It provides many good resting places, some running water, and landmarks to steer a descent through fog.

The two tracks come back together at the base of Anvil Rock. From here stay on the snowfield, heading upward and slightly left over the Muir Snowfield toward Gibraltar Rock. Usually the snowfield is deeply covered in snow and perfectly safe, but some years crevasses open. Be wary of small surface cracks—they mark the location of holes that underneath may be very wide and very deep. Only an experienced mountaineer can tell which line of progress is safe—and when there are crevasses, only experienced mountaineers equipped with rope and ice axes should proceed. At such times hikers would be well advised to turn around; in any event they should follow only the well-used tracks and definitely give up if the snow is soft around the cracks.

The view from Camp Muir is very well worth the effort. A close-up look at the Cowlitz Glacier and the rubble wall of Gibraltar. Down below, a vertical 1½km (1 mile) below, the tiny buildings at Paradise. Far off, more volcanoes—Mt. Adams and Mt. St. Helens, and a long way into Oregon, Mt. Hood and Mt. Jefferson.

Paradise Ice Caves

PARADISE AREA

46 Paradise Ice Caves

Round trip 8¾km (5½ miles)
Hiking time 3 hours
High point 1920 meters (6300 feet)
Elevation gain 335 meters (1100 feet)
Snowfree late July
   through September

Walk beneath old glacier ice and see deep blue light penetrating the roof of some of the few easily-accessible ice caves in the world. Take along plenty of clothes; even on a hot summer day, entering the caves is like stepping into a refrigerator. Better do this on a weekday—up to 1700 people have visited the caves on a single Sunday.

Note: More recent years than not, the entrance to the caves has been too deep-buried in snow for anybody to get in, even in late summer. So, before setting out, ask the ranger about the situation.

Drive to the large parking lot near the Paradise Ranger Station. The trail starts up the stone steps across from Paradise Inn, goes right, then on a paved path rounds a corner into flower fields of Edith Creek Basin. Beyond the bridge is a junction; keep right on the lower trail continuing around the basin and dropping 100 meters to a crossing of Paradise River. From here the trail climbs Mazama Ridge to a junction with the Lakes Trail (Hike 47). Stay left to the Stevens-Van Trump Memorial commemorating their ascent of Mount Rainier in 1870. At the Memorial is a junction with the Skyline Trail (Hike 44). Keep right along an old moraine. Much of this section will be across snow patches; follow the red posts. It is essential to stay on the trail; on each side there are dangerously steep snow slopes.

Size of the caves varies from year to year as the remnants of a former glacier dwindle. Formation of a cave starts with a stream flowing underneath the ice and melting a small tunnel. Warm wind sucked through the tunnel enlarges it to a cave. Eventually the roof melts and collapses.

As the cave grows, large ice flakes slowly separate from the ceiling and without warning fall to the floor. Rangers check the caves frequently and rope off dangerous areas, but conditions change rapidly. Be watchful.

To see more country, either of two alternate return routes may be taken. For one, turn north (right) onto the Skyline Trail (Hike 44) at the Stevens-Van Trump Memorial, go 1km (¾ mile) and turn left at Golden Gate, descending into Edith Creek Basin and in 2½km (1½ miles) rejoining the approach trail just above Myrtle Falls; this alternate is only ⅓km (¼ mile) longer than the approach, but requires about a hundred meters (several hundred feet) of elevation gain to Golden Gate. For another return, almost 3km (2 miles) longer, continue on the Skyline Trail to Panorama Point and then back to the starting point.

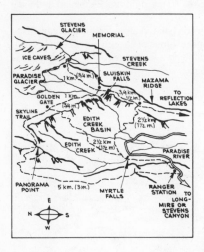

Marmot feeding in Edith Creek Basin

47 Lakes Trail

Loop trip via Wonderland Trail 7½km (4¾ miles)
Hiking time 3½ hours
High point 1765 meters (5800 feet)
Elevation gain 215 meters (700 feet)
Snowfree mid-July through September

Views, many small lakes, flowers and forests on an up-and-down walk.

Drive to the large parking lot near the Paradise Ranger Station. The trail starts across the road from Paradise Inn or at the stone steps to the left of the restrooms. The beginning 2½km (1½ miles) are identical with the Paradise Ice Caves trail (Hike 46).

The first ¾km (½ mile) to Edith Creek is paved, traversing the hill above the Inn. Cross the creek on the Myrtle Falls bridge. Keep right at the junction with the Skyline-Golden Gate Trail. The way traverses a bit higher, then drops to a crossing of the Paradise River and ascends switchbacks to Mazama Ridge. At a junction on the crest, turn right from the Paradise Ice Caves trail, following Mazama Ridge down from immense fields of flowers into alpine forest, passing numerous lakelets to a junction with an alternate section of the Wonderland Trail. Turn right, traversing slopes 150 meters (500 feet) above Reflection Lakes with views of the Tatoosh Range and the lakes, and in 2½km (1½ miles) rejoin the Lakes Trail. Turn right, dropping to the Paradise River, crossing first the highway and then the river and finally climbing back to Paradise Valley. Join the Paradise-Longmire trail a short way below the parking lot.

For a slightly longer trip, with spectacular views of Mount Rainier and Reflection Lakes, continue on the Mazama Ridge trail to Faraway Rock and tiny Artist Pool. From the brink of steep slopes beside the pool look out to the Tatoosh Range and down to the lakes. Directly below is Louise Lake. On a bench above the switchbacks on the Stevens Canyon Road is Bench Lake. To the right are Reflection and Little Reflection Lakes.

The trail descends abruptly to Little Reflection Lake. Walk along the shoulder of the road and pick up the Lakes Trail again at the first grove of trees by Reflection Lake. At the west shore is a junction. Keep right, climbing a low ridge to the rejoining of the Wonderland Trail and the return to Paradise.

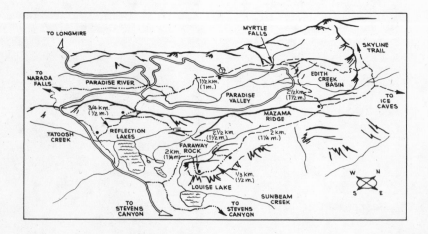

Tatoosh Range from Faraway Rock

PARADISE AREA

48 Paradise River

One-way trip from Paradise to Longmire
9½km (6 miles)
Hiking time 2½ hours
High point 1675 meters (5500 feet)
Elevation loss 850 meters (2800 feet)
Recommended July through September
Recommended from Narada Falls June
   through October

Start in alpine meadows, descend into forest, pass two waterfalls, and end up walking along the Nisqually River.

The trip can be done in either direction, of course, but is most appealing when a party arrives at Paradise and finds the weather too poor or the snow too deep for high-country strolls. In such case don't give up the day as a lost cause: take the downhill trail either from Paradise or Narada Falls and finish either at Cougar Rock Campground or Longmire. Obviously a member of the group must be willing to drive the car down; either that or someone must arrange a ride back to where the car was left.

Drive to the large parking lot near Paradise Ranger Station. (Don't confuse this with the large, modern Paradise Visitor Center.) The trail begins on the south side of the lot, just where it funnels into the one-way downhill road.

The route generally follows the Narada Ski Trail; if there is snow on the ground, watch for orange markers. In ¾km (½ mile) is a junction to the Wonderland Trail and Lakes Trail (Hike 47); keep right, descending along the Paradise River. Cross the river at Stevens Canyon Road and soon reach the Narada Falls parking lot, 2km (1¼ miles) from Paradise.

Find the paved trail, marked "Narada Falls Viewpoint," which drops rapidly within sight, sound, and spray of the falls.

The paved trail ends at the viewpoint and a fork. Continue about 150 meters (a few hundred yards) to the Wonderland Trail junction. Left are Reflection Lakes; go right, toward Longmire. If this portion of the route is snow-covered, look for orange markers on trees. In about 1½km (1 mile) from Narada Falls is a series of three bridges, the first over the Paradise River, the others over small creeks. Just before the first bridge is Paradise River Camp. The altitude is now 1160 meters (3800 feet) and large Douglas-firs appear amid the forest. At approximately 3km (2 miles) is an unmarked junction. Keep right. The left fork drops to the river and headworks of the water intake for the Park's power generator. Watch for Carter Falls on the left, hidden behind a curtain of small trees. The next 1km (¾ mile) of trail more or less parallels the huge, wooden water pipes; the figures painted on trees at intervals note the number of feet from the generator.

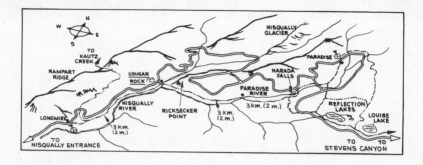

Wonderland Trail along the Nisqually River

The valley levels off rather abruptly. South are the towering cliffs of Eagle Peak; to the north is Ricksecker Point. The trail passes the generator plant and then follows the service road about ¹/₃km (¼ mile), crossing the Nisqually River close to the Paradise highway and the entrance to Cougar Rock Campground, 6½km (4 miles) from Narada Falls.

To complete the remaining 3km (2 miles) to Longmire, don't cross the highway. Find the trail near the road and continue on downhill, sometimes in sight of the river, always in pleasant moss-covered forest.

49 Van Trump Park

Round trip 8km (5 miles)
Hiking time 3 hours
High point 1676 meters (5500 feet)
Elevation gain 580 meters (1900 feet)
Snowfree mid-July
  to mid-October

One of the most beautiful waterfalls in the Park, flower-strewn meadows, a look at the Kautz Glacier, and a better-than-average chance to see mountain goats—for such reasons this ranks among Rainier's most popular hikes.

Drive 16km (10 miles) from the Nisqually Entrance toward Paradise. The trail starts from a small parking lot ¹/₃km (¼ mile) before Christine Falls, on the left side of the road before the bridge.

To the crossing of Van Trump Creek, the way is quite steep; beyond, only fairly steep. In ¾km (½ mile) the trail traverses an avalanche slope where snowslides annually tear out parts of the tread; the passage can be dangerous early in the season, when the trail is buried under a snowfield ending in wild water of the creek; it can also be dangerous after dark, even without snow.

At 2½km (1½ miles) the track crosses a fork of Van Trump Creek and soon comes in sight of Comet Falls, 98 meters (320 feet) of thunder and mist. The best view is from the first two switchbacks—of the many which begin here.

Steep walking through trees and cliffs ends suddenly at the edge of Van Trump Park, 4km (2½ miles).

The energetic hiker can continue up the ridge toward the mountain to where greenery ends and the rubble and ice of glaciers begin. The first walkers of the day often see goats here.

A good vista of the Kautz Glacier is from Mildred Point. Follow the main trail across Van Trump Creek ¾km (½ mile) to a trail junction. Mildred Point is ¾km (½ mile) uphill.

If transportation can be arranged, a loop trip can be made by returning down the Rampart Ridge trail 4km (2½ miles) to the Wonderland Trail junction. Take the left fork 2½km (1½ miles) down to Longmire (Hike 3).

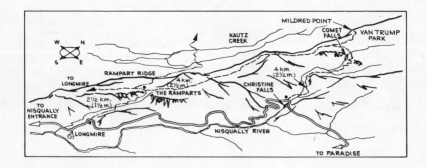

Comet Falls, 100 meters high (320 feet)

Complete loop 147km (92 miles)
Total elevation gain 6100 meters (20,000 feet)

50 The Wonderland Trail

The 147km (92-mile) Wonderland Trail completely encircles Mount Rainier, passing through every life zone of the National Park from valley forests to alpine meadows to high barrens of rock and snow. Along the way are trees, flowers, animals, and glaciers. And views: so different does Rainier look from various segments, it's difficult to recognize it as all the same mountain. As the summit of Rainier is to a climber, so the Wonderland Trail is to a hiker—the experience of a lifetime.

The entire trail can be done in a single week, and 10 days is about average. However, to allow full enjoyment of scenic highlights and opportunity for side-trips, a party should spend 2 weeks or more—not forgetting extra time for sitting out several or so days of rain. In applying for a backcountry use permit, list every camp you plan to use and the dates. If unable to keep to schedule, contact the backcountry ranger and he will help change the itinerary.

All supplies for the whole trip can be carried from the beginning, but this makes for hard, slow walking the early days. A better plan is to deposit food caches beforehand at two automobile-accessible intermediate points around the circle, or arrange to be met at these points by friends bringing the supplies. Ranger stations will store food for you. There is no place along the route to buy staples except the guide service at Paradise, which offers a few lightweight items; meals can be purchased at Sunrise, Paradise, and Longmire for a change from backpacker menus. Another alternative is to do segments of the trip in different years—though in each case transportation must be arranged to avoid doubling back.

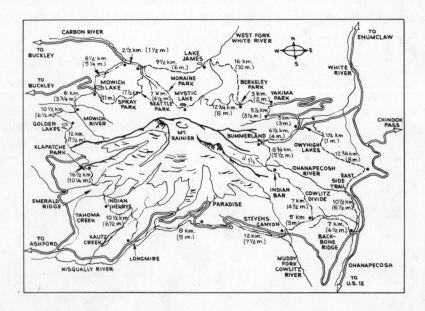

Wonderland Trail at Sunrise

Be prepared for rain by carrying a tent or tarp. Few parties are lucky enough to complete the entire trip without a few days of mist, downpour, or perhaps snow—which can and does fall on the high meadows even in summer. The occasional shelter cabins cannot be counted on; they are small and often full. Other details of equipment and planning are covered in the introduction. Camping along the trail is allowed **only** at the places specifically noted.

The Wonderland Trail is described clockwise here, but can be done either direction; one is as good as the other.

Deer in silver forest along the trail to Golden Lakes

Part 1: Longmire to Mowich Lake

One-way trip 60km (37 miles)
Allow 4-7 days
High point 1740 meters (5700 feet)
Elevation gain 2600 meters (8500 feet)
Best mid-July
    through September

The Wonderland Trail begins in forest and climbs to meadows close under the Tahoma and Puyallup Glaciers, dips into trees and rises into flowers, again and again, and traverses the entire west side of the mountain.

The first day from Longmire is to Devils Dream Creek (Hike 5), a 9½km (6-mile) walk with a total elevation gain of 884 meters (2900 feet).

The second day cross Emerald Ridge (Hike 7) and St. Andrews and Klapatche Parks to a camp at the North Puyallup River, total distance 19km (12 miles), elevation

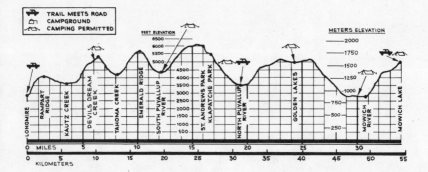

gain 975 meters (3200 feet). One might prefer to break the trip by camping at the South Puyallup River.

The third day is to Golden Lakes (Hike 9), 12km (7½ miles) and 518 meters (1700 feet). This calls for an extra day, exploring the ridge to Sunset Lookout.

The next campsite is either an easy 10½km (6½ miles) downhill to the Mowich River, a good place to stop if the weather is bad, or 6km (3¾ miles) farther and 640 meters (2100 feet) higher at Mowich Lake, a poor place to camp in the rain. The river camp is located between the north and south forks of the river.

Part 2: Mowich Lake to White River

> **One-way trip (main route) 40km (25 miles)**
> **Allow 3-6 days**
> **High point 2040 meters (6700 feet)**
> **Elevation gain 1920 meters (6300 feet)**
> **Best mid-July**
> **through September**

The second section of the Wonderland Trail rounds the cold north side of the mountain, passing under towering Willis Wall. Flower meadows and small peaks. Two alternates to the main route are available.

The first day from Mowich Lake is along the level to Ipsut Pass and steeply down to Ipsut Creek Campground (Hike 15), an easy and quick 8½km (5¼ miles) with plenty of time left over to visit Eunice Lake and Tolmie Peak (Hike 11).

The **alternate first day** is more strenuous but very rewarding. Climb through Spray Rock (Hike 12), and descend through Seattle Park (Hike 16), to Cataract Valley Camp. Total for the day, 14½km (9 miles); elevation gain, 336 meters (1200 feet). Next day drop 2½km (1½ miles) and rejoin the Wonderland Trail at the Carbon River.

The second day is from Ipsut Creek Campground through Moraine Park (Hike 18) to Mystic Lake, 9½km (6 miles) and 1188 meters (3900 feet)—a splendid walk.

The third day begins with a drop to the Winthrop Glacier, followed by a climb over Skyscraper Pass to a junction above Berkeley Park. Camping is allowed in Berkeley Park, but at a site 1½km (1 mile) off the Wonderland Trail and a good bit below. Most hikers therefore continue on to the hike-in Sunrise Campground in Yakima Park,

Berkeley Park

16km (10 miles) from Mystic Lake, elevation gain 670 meters (2200 feet). The remaining way to White River Campground is only 5km (3 miles), all downhill.

(The **alternate second and third days** also make a splendid walk—the Northern Loop described in Hike 17. From Ipsut Creek Campground it's 12km, 7½ miles, and 915 meters, 3000 feet, of elevation to the camp at Lake James; side-trips along the way to Natural Bridge and Windy Point. From Lake James to White River Campground—via a descent to the West Fork White River, a climb into Grand Park, and on through Berkeley Park and Sunrise—is 25km, 15½ miles, and 1066 meters, 3500 feet. In summary, the alternate is 4km, 2½ miles, more than the main route but 300 less meters, 1000 feet, to gain.)

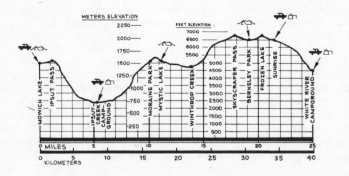

Part 3: White River to Longmire

One-way trip 53km (33 miles)
Allow 4-6 days
High point 2042 meters (6700 feet)
Elevation gain 1740 meters (5700 feet)
Best mid-July
 through September

The third and final section of the Wonderland Trail, around the east side of the mountain and back to the starting point on the south, offers still more forests, creeks, flowers, and glaciers. It traverses the highest portion of the circuit, the most likely place of all to see mountain goats.

The first day from White River Campground begins with 3km (2 miles) down the gravel road to the White River bridge. Beyond the bridge 100 meters, find the Wonderland Trail on the right side of the paved Sunrise road; in 1½km (1 mile), at Fryingpan Creek, join the Summerland trail (Hike 20) and climb 6½km (4 miles) from forest to a camp near the meadow at Summerland. Distance from White River Campground, 11km (7 miles); elevation gain, 460 meters (1500 feet).

The second day climb into rocks and snow (and goats, maybe) of 2042-meter (6700-foot) Panhandle Gap, the highest point of the Wonderland Trail, and drop to Indian Bar (Hike 40); 9½km (6 miles) walked, 853km (2800 feet) gained.

The third day is 10½km (6½ miles) to a camp at Nickel Creek, mostly downhill but with some 250 meters (800 feet) of elevation to gain along the up-and-down crest of the upper Cowlitz Divide. Alternately, to make the next day easier, continue 3km (2 miles) to Maple Creek Camp.

The fourth day is long and arduous and not entirely pleasant. Hike 1½km (1 mile) to the Stevens Canyon Road at Box Canyon, cross the bridge and drop some 100 meters and then begin a 12km (7½-mile) climb along Stevens Creek to Reflection Lakes. Make an early start: the heat can be unbearable; even in shadows of morning one can feel heat reflecting from the barren, burned-off opposite side of the canyon. Maybe the worst thing for morale is the stream of automobiles speeding along the Stevens Canyon Road, never out of sight or sound. Still there are rewards, including clear waters (and the camp) of Maple Creek. Sylvia Falls is a nice surprise, and also cool and refreshing Martha Falls—actually a series of falls (the most interesting one is 100 meters above the trail). From Martha Creek the trail ascends another steep 1½km (mile), crosses the road, and climbs on to Louise Lake and Reflection Lakes. From the lakes a hiker has a choice. One alternative is to follow the Wonderland Trail above Reflection Lakes, turning left just past Faraway Rock, proceeding over Mazama Ridge to Paradise Valley, crossing the Paradise River, and joining the Paradise-Longmire trail (Hike 48) ¾km (½ mile) below Paradise and 8¾km (5½ miles) above Longmire. The shorter alternative is to hike the road 1½km (1 mile) from Reflection Lakes to the Paradise-Longmire trail. Drop along Paradise River below Narada Falls (1½km, 1 mile below which is Paradise Camp), follow the river under Ricksecker Point and past the powerhouse to Cougar Rock Campground and then another 3km (2 miles) to Longmire. On the shorter alternative the total distance for the last lap from Nickel Creek to Longmire is 21½km (13½ miles), 640 meters (2100 feet) of elevation gained.

(If party inexperience or wintry conditions make it necessary or desirable to avoid Panhandle Gap, an alternate route is available from Fryingpan Creek to Box Canyon via Owyhigh Lakes, Hike 19; the East Side Trail, Hike 33; and Cowlitz Divide, Hike 38. Camps near Owyhigh Lakes and Deer Creek. Totals for the alternate are 32km, 20

Martha Falls

miles, and 1160 meters, 3800 feet of elevation, compared to 23km (14½ miles) and 1160 meters, 3800 feet, on the section of the Wonderland Trail for which it substitutes.)

The hiker who arrives back at Longmire, having hiked 147km (92 miles) plus side-trips, having gained some 6100 meters (20,000 feet) or more, can feel proud. His accomplishment is as impressive as climbing to the summit of Rainier—and in many ways he has come to know the mountain more intimately than any climber. He will be most aware of the many ways in which he and the mountain and its plants and animals are interrelated. He will find, as John Muir did, that, "When we try to pick out anything by itself, we find it hitched to everything else in the universe."

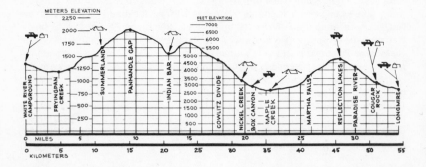

Patrol cabin at Indian Henrys Hunting Ground

RECOMMENDED READING

Trips and Trails, 2: Family Camps, Short Hikes, and View Roads in the Olympics, Mt. Rainier and the South Cascades, (Second ed.) E.M. Sterling and Bob and Ira Spring. The Mountaineers. Seattle; 1978.

Exploring Mount Rainier, Ruth Kirk. University of Washington Press. Seattle and London; 1968.

Geology of Mount Rainier National Park, Washington, Richard S. Fiske, Clifford A. Hopson, and Aaron C. Waters. Geological Survey Professional Paper 444. United States Government Printing Office, Washington; 1963.

Cascade Alpine Guide, Columbia River to Stevens Pass, Fred Beckey. The Mountainers, Seattle; 1974.

Mountaineering, The Freedom of the Hills. The Mountaineers. Seattle; fourth edition, 1982.

Backpacking: One Step at a Time, Harvey Manning. Random, New York; 1981.

The Challenge of Rainier, Dee Molenaar. The Mountaineers. Seattle; third edition, 1979.

TIME OF YEAR MOST SUITABLE FOR HIKING

Recommended time for hiking means the time of year the trail is generally free of snow. From year to year this varies a week or more, and for a few weeks after the recommended time, snow patches can be expected on the trail. Above 5000 feet snowstorms occasionally occur in July, August, and September. However, the snow usually melts in a few hours or a day.

MOST OF THE YEAR
 2 Longmire Woods Trails
10 Paul Peak Loop (lower section)
13 Rain Forest Nature Trail

SNOWFREE IN MAY
 3 Rampart Ridge
13 Carbon River Trails
35 Grove of the Patriarchs
36 Three Lakes Trail (first mile)
37 Silver Falls
48 Narada to Longmire

JUNE
10 Paul Peak Loop
14 Green Lake
15 Ipsut Creek
25 Huckleberry Creek
   (from bottom)
29 Crystal Lakes
33 East Side Trail
34 Shriner Peak

EARLY JULY
 1 Eagle Peak
 7 Emerald Ridge
 9 Golden Lakes
19 Owyhigh Lakes
20 Summerland
21 Glacier Basin
36 Three Lakes Trail
38 Cowlitz Divide
39 Backbone Ridge

41 Bench and Snow Lakes
43 Nisqually Vista
44 Skyline Trail
48 Paradise to Longmire

MID-JULY
 4 Kautz Creek Trail
 5 Indian Henrys Hunting Ground
 8 Klapatche Park
11 Tolmie Park
12 Spray Park
16 Seattle Park
17 Northern Loop
18 Moraine Park
22 Palisades Lakes
23 Sunrise Nature Trails
24 Sourdough Mountains
25 Huckleberry Creek (top)
26 Mt. Fremont Lookout
27 Grand Park
28 Burroughs Mountain
30 Deadwood Lakes
31 Naches Peak
32 Pacific Crest Trail
40 Indian Bar
43 Paradise Flower Trails
47 Lakes Trail
49 Van Trump Park

AUGUST
42 Pinnacle Saddle
46 Ice Caves

INDEX

OTHER BOOKS IN THE "HIKES" SERIES:

50 Hikes in Mount Rainier National Park
101 Hikes in the North Cascades
102 Hikes in the Alpine Lakes, South Cascades and Olympics
Companion volumes guide you to the best hiking in the mountains of Washington State . . . valleys and ridges, forests, glacier views, subalpine meadows, ice caves and snowfields. Easy-to-use sketch maps and complete trail directions. "101" covers from Stevens Pass to the Canadian Border. "102" covers from Stevens Pass south to the Columbia River. "50" includes the Wonderland Trail and Mount Rainier. Text by Harvey Manning, photos by Bob and Ira Spring.

103 Hikes in Southwestern British Columbia
The most scenic trips from Vancouver Island to Manning Park, from the U.S. Border to Lytton at the head of the Fraser Canyon. (Includes Garibaldi Park.) Maps and photos for each trip. Prepared by the B.C. Mountaineering Club, with text by David Macaree, maps by Mary Macaree.

109 Walks in B.C.'s Lower Mainland
Delightful walks to see the best in Vancouver and vicinity. Complete directions and maps for each trip; scenic photos of the highlights. Text by David Macaree, photos by Mary Macaree.

Trips and Trails, 1: Family Camps, Short Hikes and View Roads Around the North Cascades
Trips and Trails, 2: Family Camps, Short Hikes and View Roads in the Olympics, Mt. Rainier and South Cascades
Companion volumes geared for beginner hikers and families, with maps, photos and complete trail directions for short hikes (under two miles) starting from campgrounds. Also describes facilities of each campground. "1" includes the San Juan, Whidbey and Fidalgo Island areas. By E.M. Sterling, photos by Bob and Ira Spring, maps by Marge Mueller.

Bicycling the Backroads Around Puget Sound
Bicycling the Backroads of Northwest Washington
Bicycling the Backroads of Southwest Washington
Full details, maps on cycle tours on quiet backroads, including scenery, mileages, elevation change, estimated times. Companion volumes, no duplication of trips. By Erin and Bill Woods.

The photographers' favorite picture, "Little Valley Pounder," taken near St. Andrews Park in 1950 as Terry Spring follows his mother's footsteps

BOOKS FROM THE MOUNTAINEERS

50 Hikes in Mount Rainier National Park
101 Hikes in the North Cascades
102 Hikes in the Alpine Lakes, South Cascades and Olympics
103 Hikes in Southwestern British Columbia
109 Walks in B.C.'s Lower Mainland
Trips and Trails, 1: Family Camps, Short Hikes and View Roads Around the North Cascades
Trips and Trails, 2: Family Camps, Short Hikes and View Roads in the Olympics, Mt. Rainier and South Cascades
Bicycling the Backroads Around Puget Sound
Bicycling the Backroads of Northwest Washington
Discover Southeast Alaska with Pack and Paddle
55 Ways to the Wilderness in Southcentral Alaska
Hikers' Map to the North Cascades: Routes and Rocks in the Mt. Challenger Quadrangle
Guide to Leavenworth Rock Climbing Areas
Cascade Alpine Guide: Climbing and High Routes, Columbia River to Stevens Pass
Cascade Alpine Guide: Climbing and High Routes, Stevens Pass to Rainy Pass
Climbers' Guide to the Olympic Mountains
Darrington and Index: Rock Climbing Guide
Snow Trails: Ski and Snowshoe Routes in the Cascades
Mountaineering: The Freedom of the Hills
Medicine for Mountaineering
Mountaineering First Aid
Snowshoeing
The South Cascades: The Gifford Pinchot National Forest
The Unknown Mountain
Fire and Ice: The Cascade Volcanoes
Across the Olympic Mountains: The Press Expedition
Men, Mules and Mountains: Lieutenant O'Neil's Olympic Expeditions
The Coffee Chased Us Up: Monte Cristo Memories
Challenge of the North Cascades
Bicycling Notes
Hiking Notes
Climbing Notes
Mountains of the World
Northwest Trees
The Ascent of Denali
Storm and Sorrow in the High Pamirs
Canoe Routes: Yukon Territory
Canoe Routes: British Columbia
Footsore, 1: Walks and Hikes Around Puget Sound
Footsore, 2: Walks and Hikes Around Puget Sound
Hikers/Climbers Maps of Monte Cristo, Glacier Peak
Tales of a Western Mountaineer

Send for illustrated catalog.